Newcomer

ISBN 978-0-557-28070-4

Printed in the United States of America

Author contact: ballagasmanny52@aol.com

Dedicated to my parents, my son, my wife, and the United States,
the country that changed my life

Newcomer
An American
Adventure

Manuel Ballagas

Foreword

THEY SAY AMERICA IS a country of immigrants. Yet many complain often about us here, both in private and in the public square. We are blamed for many things, from trying to impose our language on unwilling communities to altering "the nation's social fabric" beyond recognition.

Welcome to the world of nativists, who similarly complained of the Irish, Italian and Chinese immigrants who preceded us. What can we do about it? Poor souls, they underestimate the enormous capacity America has to alter –way beyond recognition- those lucky enough to arrive on its shores.

In fact, nearly three decades after I moved to this country, I am not, by far, the same man who got off a boat in Key West with his family and the scarce belongings we brought with us in our only suitcase. Surely, I have changed much, and with God's help and our own efforts, for the better

The columns in this book describe the painful –and often comical- process of immersion in the habits and demands of my land of adoption. They were not intended to move to tears or laughter; only to induce a hopeful smile in those who must now struggle to overcome the numerous obstacles and apparent enigmas that haunt immigrants in America.

I began to write these articles in June 2005, while my wife and I were getting ready to return to sunny Florida, where one of the most exciting professional challenges in my life was waiting for me. After spending almost eight years in the chills of New York, where I worked as the news editor of *The Wall Street Journal Américas*, I had great anticipation and very good feelings about this move.

As a result, perhaps, my message ended up being so positive. Quite a number of readers told me at some point that my columns had helped them understand that, even if the United States is no easy ride, in the end those who persevere and refuse to give up obtain the measure of success they deserve.

A number of these articles were published originally in Spanish, in *Tu Dinero*, a monthly personal finance magazine directed by my good friend, Colombian-born journalist Jaime Mejía Mazuera; the rest, I published myself in *CENTRO Tampa*, the Spanish-language weekly I launched and directed for four years in that historic city in West Florida.

Now, closer to retirement and, I presume, a less stressful life, I decided to put these pieces together in book form, in the hope they may inspire and encourage those who, like myself years ago, are newcomers to this wonderful country.

Better a good friend than a resume

EVERY TIME I LISTEN to someone whine about how difficult life is in America, I can't help but smile. It's not that I feel glad about it; it's just that I remember how many times I whined about it myself. As a newcomer, I was so clueless I had no idea how to find a job in this country.

My resume was a total disaster. To begin with, none of the information it provided about me was verifiable in the United States. Growing increasingly desperate, I turned to the patron saint of many Latin Americans like myself –the government.

The state employment agency occupied a huge building close to other similar shrines of bureaucracy in the town where I lived at the time. Since many flocked there to process their unemployment benefits, Latinos had coined a "Spanglish" term for it –the *desemployment* office. A job bank also operated there, where many hopefuls applied for dozens of positions in the state government.

A lady who was in charge of the office decided I might be qualified for a job as a driver's license examiner. I explained I didn't even have a license myself yet, but she insisted that was unimportant. However, she warned me I would have to pass several tests, including one to assess my typing skills.

Even if I've always been a lousy typist, I passed the test in my third try. But the flood of junk mail and terse notifications I got in return for all my efforts only added to my disappointment. No decent lead developed from this search. After a while, I concluded the government had pulled a fast one on me.

What a difficult life this is, I kept telling myself. I had arrived in the country several months before, and I was standing in a bus stop, with just a couple bucks in my pocket and wishing for a lightning to strike me then and there, when someone suddenly spoke to me.

I turned around and saw him. He was a short man in some kind of funny uniform. He asked me if I was a newcomer looking for a job. When I told him I was, he offered to recommend me to the restaurant where he worked as a waiter. They were hiring dishwashers. "It pays $4 an hour," he said. I didn't think it twice.

I was euphoric when I got back home that afternoon, but my wife only frowned. In our country, washing dishes is the epitome of failure. I felt, however, victorious. I was sure this could be the threshold to a top position in a large chain of five-star hotels.

Then, suddenly, the phone rang. A friend was calling to tell me there was an "opening" in the newspaper where his wife was working at the time. It wasn't a newsroom position, of course, but at least I would be close to the paper and the ink I loved so much.

"And what would I be doing in this job exactly?" I asked.

"Paste-up," my friend said.

I soon discovered this was one of the most boring and tedious tasks in the business back in the 80's: basically pasting shiny strips of computer-generated matter on the paper's empty templates. But at least I would have a job –and even health insurance.

Since then, I've held several jobs, each one a better paid one than the one before. I don't whine so much either. On the contrary, I count myself as lucky to be living in America. I have reached impressive landmarks in my profession, too. My skills and perseverance certainly helped, as well as my unshakeable faith in God and myself. But you know what? I have a good friend to thank for every job I've had in this country.

A parker's license

BACK WHERE I CAME FROM, owning a car was as a status symbol. The only one in my family who owned one was my uncle, whom I used to call "Uncle Pupu". Every time he visited, it was like a party for me, because he let me sit at the wheel of his shiny Buick and make it honk: "Pu-pu... Pu-pu". That's the closest I ever came to driving a car, and it never crossed my mind that I would need a driver's license some day.

But as soon as I arrived in America, the first thing my cousin told me was I would need to find myself a car, and drive. For better or for worse, I had to admit he was right. In that town, you could very well die of old age waiting for a bus. Believe me, it almost happened to me several times.

I began by getting a temporary, or learner's, license. I easily passed the written test, but the road test was a different story.

If you want to learn how to drive and you have no one to teach you free of charge, your best bet is a driving school. In that town, everyone learned with Mi Tío Driving School. It was very popular, especially among newcomers like me. Many of the teachers were Latinos and spoke Spanish. Besides, it was very cheap.

14

My teacher at Mi Tío turned out to be an Argentinean lady. She drove to pick me up at home, and immediately made me sit at the wheel. I thought she was going to explain some basic things first and then show me how to operate the vehicle, but instead she ordered me to start the engine and drive right away.

Who? Me? Drive?

I gulped, but refusing her instruction was out of the question. I didn't want this woman to see me as a wimp. So I turned the ignition, very macho-like, shifted to "drive", let go of the brake, and quietly stepped on the gas. Oh, what a rush! Believe me, nothing compares to moving through this world at 40 miles per hour.

Almost unaware of it, I learned how to drive. I thought that would be enough, but as I soon found out, in order to be a good driver you must not only move ahead without running over other human beings or crashing into other cars. Above all, you must learn to park. You know, bring the car to a stop at a certain place and in a certain way.

It's easier said than done, because parallel parking can be an extraordinary, quasi-sublime feat at times. The driver is required to slide his vehicle backward, between two cars so close to each other they might as well be Siamese twins.

As much as I tried, I failed miserably at this all the time. My teacher did her best, but it soon became apparent it was a waste of time. Finally, she gave up on me and wished me luck in my road test. She advised me to seek the help of St. Jude, a very powerful saint, according to her.

But even with the saint's intercession I failed the test five times in a row. I did all turns the right way, and I stopped, as required, at every sign on the road. But as soon as I had to park, my test went all the way south.

Crazy with frustration, I went for another test. It was a hot day, but while I waited for my turn, I saw the skies turn gray and stormy. A bunch of very fortunate applicants had already passed their tests and were running off to get their pictures taken for their driver's licenses. How I wished to be in their shoes!

Finally, my name was called. A lightning suddenly crossed the sky and a deafening thunder was heard, too.

I hired an old Ford from one of many driving schools that were doing business there, and soon I was taking the test. Then, it started raining cats and dogs. Close by, under the rain, I saw the two fatal little sticks between which I would have to park, and I clearly saw myself being flunked again. But I got a reprieve. The examiner told me we would need to wait for the rain to stop

And so we waited, watching the rain and the wind lash at the little sticks mercilessly. After a while, the rain stopped, and the examiner said, "Let's go."

The little sticks were still standing, but they were so far apart from each other, a truck could have easily fit between them. I thought the examiner would return them to their place again, but he didn't take the trouble to do that. I suspect he was in a hurry to leave.

Quickly, I started the car, drove close to the little sticks and slid in reverse into the wide, comfortable space Mother Nature had opened for me. "Test passed, congratulations," the examiner said.

Since then, I've held licenses in several states. I drive happily, and at times, I must admit, with a touch of imprudence; but never again have I parked a car in parallel. I couldn't, even if my life depended on it. Just between you and I, I haven't learned to do it yet.

How I won my first lawsuit
without even trying

THIS IS A NATION OF LAWS... and lawsuits. Suing is practically a basic human right in America. Anyone, from a humble worker to a movie star, is entitled to seek legal remedy for any grievance before this country's courts. The payoffs can be, at times, in the order of millions; the causes are often trivial.

As a newcomer, I had no idea how to bring a lawsuit. Not that I was interested in doing that either. I've never been inclined to slip in stores or fall down a flight of stairs in someone else's home –all of which seem to be strict requirements to initiate legal action in this country.

To be left crippled or disfigured would be reason enough to sue in any part of the world, but in America it's not uncommon to declare yourself the victim of someone's clumsiness for any reason at all. A coconut falls on your head, so you bring a lawsuit against the city you're living in. Or you run to find yourself a neck brace the minute you realize you've crashed into a tycoon's limousine, so you can collect for your pain and suffering. Small wonder so many people here seem all too eager to be injured. It's like the lottery. Anyone can get lucky, sometimes even without buying a ticket! I know it from personal experience.

Some years ago, my wife and I were hunting for a cheap apartment in Miami. We were in a hurry. We had just moved from Washington DC and wanted a safe place to live, and one that would not break our pockets, considering my meager income as a journalist.

We canvassed the area and found a pretty apartment complex, where a Hispanic lady showed us a two-bedroom model that instantly charmed us. We were about to sign the lease when another lady in the rental office intervened. She told us there were no apartments available at the moment and that we would be placed on a waiting list. We left the place very disappointed, but a few days later we found a house with a huge yard full of mango and avocado trees. We forgot all about the apartment, but life in this country is full of surprises.

Two years later, I was browsing in my computer at work, looking for the stories the *Herald* would run next morning, when I came across an interesting piece: the owners of an apartment complex had been found guilty of discriminating Black and Latino rental applicants, and ordered to pay the hefty sum of $4.5 million. It was the same complex where we had gone shortly after moving from Washington. The story ran in the paper, together with a form issued by the U.S. Attorney's Office, so all those affected could fill it out and claim a part of the proceeds.

We quickly filled the form and put it in the mail. We always had our suspicions about that incident, but we had never dreamed of suing. What for? We were too busy making a life for ourselves and legal things tend to become so messy. Yet it seems there was actually something to that funny feeling we had.

The company's files were full of documents in which potential tenants were identified either by the color of their skin or their accented English. If they did not pass the color and language tests, they were doomed to the proverbial waiting list —a very long one, of course. How idiotic. They made it so easy for the prosecutors to prove their case and for us to get a fat check in the mail —tax free, by the way.

Although there was actually a single litigant, many shared in that lawsuit, including us. We got our part -$15,000- more or less close to Thanksgiving, which gave us all the more reason to be thankful that year. That's what Americans call a class-action suit, and we had unwittingly become a part of one.

As someone famous said once, what a country!

I owe, therefore I exist

BACK WHERE I CAME FROM, it's a sin to be in debt. In America, if you don't owe at least some money, you are basically an outcast. That's how it is. You cannot make plane or hotel reservations over the phone, nor buy a car, much less obtain a mortgage to finance your own house. It's a veritable handicap. Tell me about it.

As a newcomer, one of the first things that caught my attention was those shiny plastic pieces called credit cards. I just loved the elegant gesture with which people dropped them on a table to pay the bill in a restaurant. Or the casual manner with which they handed them over to a cashier to close on a more or less extravagant purchase in a department store.

I didn't understand the logic behind these transactions, but a relative explained each time you pay with a credit card it's as if a bank gave you a loan on the spot. He then advised me to get a card as soon as possible. "You can't afford not to have credit in this country," he said.

Right away, I began applying for all sorts of credit cards. Every time I found an application form in an old magazine, I filled it out and put it in the mail. I would receive a terse, polite refusal a few days later, and the reason seemed to be always the same —my insufficient, or rather non-existent, credit. I had arrived in America barely a year before, I was working and paying all my bills on time, but I didn't owe anyone a penny. It was as if I didn't exist.

"They don't give you a card because you have no credit history, but you don't have a credit history because they don't give you a card," a pessimistic friend told me one day. He had resigned himself to pay in cash for all his purchases.

It was like that old enigma —who came first, the egg or the chicken? But I was bent on deciphering it, so I went ahead and continued sending applications to those elusive giants —Visa, MasterCard and American Express.

One afternoon, I was walking through an upscale Ohio store, visually absorbing the costly items that were sold there, when my eyes fell on a beautiful wristwatch. I was so mesmerized by it, a store employee had to wake me up. She asked if she could help me, and since I had the rest of the day off, I asked her to show me the impressive timepiece. I put it on my wrist, admired it for a moment then quietly returned it.

The employee must have guessed my state of mind, because she immediately offered me a credit card application form, insisting that if I filled it out, I would be able to buy the wristwatch of my dreams —on a month-to-month basis, that is. I did so, and I left the store with a smile.

I was convinced I would soon be denied as usual, but some days later an envelope from the store came in the mail. This time, it was a little fatter and heavier. The minute I opened it, my hands began to shake. Surprise, surprise. Inside, there was a shiny plastic card with my name embossed on it! It came with a rather pathetic line of credit, but that very afternoon, my wife and I ran off to the store to do some shopping. I was already on my way to be happily in debt.

Someone explained later that this happened sometimes. Department stores, especially the high end ones, tend to extend credit more easily because they charge huge interest rates. Gas companies are also less demanding, I was told. So in a matter of weeks I already had another card with which I could fill my car's tank without using cash. How exciting!

Twenty years plus later, I have more credit cards than I can fit in my wallet, and I turn up on the radar of every reporting agency. Not a week goes by when I don't get new offers in the mail. I only have to worry about paying on time for all I owe, and of not owing too much, of course. Those are the rules. I owe; therefore, I exist.

A new life calls for a new car

THE STORY OF MY CARS resembles very much that of my life in America.

The first car I owned was a *tiburón*, or shark. We called it that because it was very long and had a kind of pointy nose, like those dreadful, carnivorous fishes of the Caribbean. Luckily, mine had no teeth, perhaps because he was very old already. The best was he had come very cheap, about $400 cash. You couldn't ask for more.

The guy who sold it to me told me proudly, "You got yourself a great car there, Manny." He should have added it would not be for a very long time, because that cute shark of mine lasted barely four months in my possession. It quietly expired one afternoon, as I was turning a corner close to home. I don't know what happened. It suddenly stopped, made a weird noise, and a white cloud blew from its snout. It never moved again. I had to sell it at a steep loss –for a mere 100 bucks.

Next week, I bought another car, less older than my previous one, but equally long and pointy, a true *tiburón*. I paid in cash again. It was an eight cylinder, weighed two and a half tons, and was a voracious gas-guzzler, too, but I didn't care at all. I'd never had a car like that in my life.

That car took me from Miami to Ohio, and then back to Miami, when I lost my job up there. It was spacious and had an air of elegance, but one day something terrible happened to it – the brakes quit on me. As much as I stepped on the pedal, that huge chunk of metal refused to stop. Luckily, this didn't happen in a freeway, and I was able to get close to a curb as soon as the car lost momentum. It was a close call. I almost had to give the car away shortly afterward.

Later on, I bought a very peculiar car. It must have been four or fives years old and was relatively well maintained, but as soon as you started it, it made lots of funny noises. This didn't bother me at first, but then I grew concerned it may have some kind of hidden engine problem and leave me stranded on the road when I least expected it.

A friend who was more or less a mechanic took a look at it and concluded it was in top shape, so he advised me to turn the radio on very high every time the car began to make noises. Better to listen to Willy Chirino than to a mad, clunking symphony.

By the way, at the time I was driving around without insurance. I just couldn't afford it, and if I'd had an accident I would have found myself in a real mess, but fortunately I never crashed into anyone. As they say in Spanish, God watches over the innocent.

The first insurance I had to buy was when I got into my first new car deal –a Japanese one. We lived in Washington at the time. I was working at my first serious job and I decided it was time to make my life more complicated. My credit history was so ridiculous the dealer thought it wise to warn me if I missed just one payment he would go after me and find me, no matter where I hid. I was shaken, but took the car.

I haven't driven any "sharks" since then. Some cars have lasted more than others, because I have grown fond of them. But as soon as they start breaking down or making funny noises I don't run to a mechanic or turn the radio on anymore. I just go to a reputable dealer in search of better wheels. No matter what they say, there's no sweeter scent than that of a brand new car. Ask anyone.

All over the place

MOVING IS SOMETHING that happens very often in America. I doubt people change residence so much in other parts of the world, especially in search of a better job. In this country, one spends a lot of the time going from here to there and vice versa. It's like a non-stop merry-go-round.

As a newcomer, I thought I'd never be packing my stuff again. The weather where we lived was warm, and we spent a lot of our time in the company of relatives, friends and palm trees. I had a job, a car, feasted on roast pork almost every week, and life in general seemed to smile on me. But I also wanted to make more money, of course. I was making only $8 an hour at the time. I barely could pay my bills!

The first time, we moved to Ohio. A company that published Spanish-language textbooks offered me a position there, with a relatively decent salary at the time, good benefits and a chance for advancement. So the prospects of cold weather didn't deter us, and soon we were heading up north.

We spent almost two years in the quiet, baseball-famous town of Cincinnati, believing we had reached our final destination, but we were in for a big chimichanga and taco surprise.

The Mexican peso was plummeting at the time, and though I never quite understood how the ups and downs of any currency south of the border could affect our peaceful life in that part of the Ohio Valley, the fact is the company cut its Spanish operations dramatically, and all of a sudden I found myself unemployed. That's the global economy for you.

I tried selling Latino food door to door for a time. I made some money, but truth be told, I'm not cut out to run a *bodega* on wheels, much less to plow through the snow carrying bags of food for other people. So after a couple months we decided it was time to head back to Florida.

Catching the sun again was nice, but warm weather alone hardly feeds your pockets. My job at a local radio station didn't pay that much either. Heck, I almost qualified for food stamp benefits again! Fortunately, after a time, just when I was starting to whine about having moved, I got a job offer from one of the most secure industries there is –the U.S. government. So, one fine day we flew all the way to Washington DC, courtesy of Uncle Sam.

We have moved quite a lot since then, but I have no regrets about it. Each move has meant, besides a risk, one step higher in the steep ladder of professional advancement.

By moving I got to be a part of the team that launched *El Nuevo Herald,* one of the most important daily Spanish newspapers in the country. By moving, also, I got to work in one of the world's most prestigious newspapers, *The Wall Street Journal.* Then, I returned to Florida again where I launched *The Tampa Tribune's* first Spanish-language weekly, and then lead its staff for several years. Sometimes, I just had to pinch myself. Could this be true? I could hardly believe it.

Some would probably say this has been too much moving, and they may be right. In fact, I know of many hard working people who have prospered without engaging in this sort of nomadic behavior. They have dug in, stayed firmly in one place, and have managed, nonetheless, to improve their lives in America.

Others have started profitable businesses in the first town they set foot in this country. It's admirable, but they have been most fortunate. Guys like me have no choice but to keep their suitcases ready all the time, and to follow the winding path drawn by the goddess Economy. You are seldom a prophet in your own land.

Happy and undocumented

HONESTLY, GUYS. Who hasn't been an illegal in this country at one point or another? Let him cast the first stone. No one is born into this world with a clean certificate of residence in his pocket. Things become more complicated when you cross a country's border, and if it's the U.S. border, things can get far more complicated.

Cubans like myself have some leeway. It's a matter of getting on a boat, clinging to a bridge or requesting political asylum in an airport. If you're not running away from Fidel, then you must find yourself a sponsor or wade through a rough river with the help of the Virgin of Guadalupe. Or worse: You may even have to marry the most ugly woman in the world, like a friend of mine had to do.

As a newcomer in America, I was handed a small piece of paper. It was so thin and frail I didn't dare to carry it on myself most of the time. That said it contained my name and a stamp authorizing me to be employed. It had to be renewed every year, but why would I care about that?

After a time, I came to believe I actually lived here. I worked and paid my taxes, so it was logical to assume I was a U.S. resident. I was so wrong!

One time, I decided to register for some courses in a local community college, and when I went to make the required payment, the employee in the bursar's office hit me with a ridiculously high fee.

"Why?" I cried.

"Because you are not a resident," she explained.

I was livid. I had been living for two years in that town and I could easily prove it. But the employee stubbornly refused to accept me as a resident. According to her, no matter how much time I lived anywhere, my permanence here was as thin and frail as the little paper I had been given. I lacked status. I wasn't a resident, a citizen, an inhabitant —or anything, for that matter. And I would have to pay $360 —cash or credit card, please?

Suddenly, college didn't seem such a good idea.

Later on, while we were on a trip, we thought it would be nice to do some sightseeing in Canada. It was on a whim —and a gross mistake as well. We were in Niagara Falls and someone had told us the falls looked so much better from the Canadian side, so we headed for a border crossing, where we had a run-in with one of the Migra's many foot soldiers.

"As far as I'm concerned, go ahead," he said, after taking a quick look at our documents. "But you get stuck in Canada."

When we asked why, he lost his cool.

"This is nothing!" He retorted, waving our little papers. For a while, I thought he was going to rip them apart.

"Look," he said then, as if lecturing some children. "You are basically guests here. If you leave the house, you can't get back in, understand?"

Of course we did. We retreated quietly, having decided by then we would rather watch the falls safely from the American side. It seemed healthier, too.

I suppose many newcomers could relate to such experiences – and even worse ones. There are those who don't even have a little paper like mine to show around, or the one they have seems to expire every five minutes. The seas of bureaucracy can be rocky. And it's easy to capsize in this soup of letters and numbers: I-94, H1B, I-130, H2B... It sounds like advanced algebra –and not all of us are so good at math.

So I held on to my little paper for several years. I took very good care of it. After some time, it had become as thin as a piece of ancient parchment. Finally, after what seemed an eternity, I was allowed to trade the guest card for the key to the house. I had to fill out a bunch of forms, have an X-Ray taken, but one fine day I got my green card in the mail. Come to think of it, I can count myself as very lucky. At least, I didn't have to marry the most ugly woman in the world.

Flirting with Lady Luck

I HAVE A VERY COLORFUL RELATIVE who loves attending funerals more than anything else in this world. He describes himself as a "funeral parlor rat". He runs off to every mournful ceremony that comes his way, whether of a distant relative or a mere acquaintance. "I'm just like that, Manny," he told me once. "It's my duty to them!"

Not all of us share my relative's dark predilections. What's more, if you're like me, most likely you won't want to hear any talk about death, much less during lunch. Forget it. We all know we'll be gone some day, but meanwhile, in this huge waiting room that the world is, we'd rather leaf through a magazine or watch TV while our turn comes. Why anticipate the inevitable?

So, as a newcomer in America, I firmly decided to avoid those harbingers of tragedy, life insurance sales people. It was difficult to elude them; they are almost everywhere. Even some Latinos have joined their ranks.

They turn up when you least expect it, always with an obvious piece of information at the tip of their tongues –you will kick the bucket some day, so prepare. They even tell you in Spanish! Every time I saw them come in somewhere, I ran out the door. Honestly, who would want to listen to tales of the crypt when you just started a new life in this country?

I was still living in Ohio at the time. There were very few Hispanics in my town. Gringos, as we know, contemplate death from a more practical angle. They prepare for the Great Beyond with the same diligence they get ready for a road trip or save up toward a down payment on a property. So life insurance salesmen felt very much at home there. For a while, I managed to prevail over them, even brandishing at times the argument of immortality. But fate had another surprise in store for me.

One day, my boss brought a funny visitor to the office. He was a young guy, a buddy from his college days, I think. Very friendly, like many people in the Midwest. Right off the bat, he told us he was a life insurance salesman. I had to fight an almost irrepressible impulse to run away, but all I did was to refuse his card.

"You're barking up the wrong tree," I told him.

The poor man was perplexed. He asked me why I said that.

"Look," I answered. "In case you don't know, we Latinos hate to talk about death. Quite frankly, your business is scary."

The guy just laughed.

"No one has probably explained how things really work," he said. Then, he asked me if I would have lunch with him.

I've never been the one to refuse a free meal, so after a while we were both sitting in a restaurant, taking care of two sizeable portions of fried chicken. Between bites, the Gringo salesman boiled down the thorny issue of life insurance to an amusing game of chance. I listened intently.

"Every month, when you pay your premium, you're betting $40 in the hope that you will win the $100,000 I'm betting on your good health," he explained.

I was puzzled. "What if I actually die?" I asked.

The guy shrugged.

"You never know," he said. "But with my policy, if you live to be 60, I'll give you $20,000 and the game is over."

In truth, I had never looked at it that way. And quite frankly, I was seduced by the prospects of entering old age with all that additional money.

"So where do I have to sign?" I asked.

Since then, I haven't left the game table. I have put money stubbornly on my own demise, each time for higher stakes. At my age, the game has become riskier but decidedly more exciting. Who knows? I may win the jackpot one of these days. Flirting with Lady Luck is always a good idea.

You're the boss!

I ONCE HAD A SUPERVISOR FROM HELL. I'm sure you all have had one of your own. But mine was really special, I think. Even to give you a raise he felt compelled to offer you some obnoxious comment. "I hope I don't live to regret this," he told me as he signed off on the tiny increase we were all getting that year at the *Herald*.

As a newcomer in this country, I thought I had forever left behind the tyranny of mediocre, arrogant supervisors. But I was wrong. It seems that power –and not even absolute power- eats up sometimes what little brain the top bananas ever had. America is no exception. Big corporations absorb these creeps with delight. Don't ask me why. They're like a plague.

My boss certainly was of the infernal persuasion. He would suddenly go into fits of rage for no apparent reason, and if he felt like it, he would shower you with insults in the presence of all your co-workers. Sometimes, at a safe distance, we would watch him hit his head against the walls in his office and pull his hair, in an apparent argument with himself. He was a real maniac!

It was sad –but understandable- that when he became ill, we would all pray for his slowest recuperation. Even if we never actually wished for him to leave this world, the fact that we didn't have to see him come in the door every morning was a source of great relief for all of us.

Fed up with having to deal with this gentleman and his temper tantrums, I decided to try my luck elsewhere. Fortunately, those were good times and I found a much better job soon, in one of the most prestigious newspapers in the world. Not thinking twice, I accepted the offer and got ready to move again. My wife must be angel; I don't know how she agreed to it.

In my last day of work, I found myself alone with my boss in the room where we held our afternoon news budget meetings. While we waited for the other editors to come in, my boss felt the need to tell me how much I would regret leaving for greener pastures. "Now you'll see what it's like to be waiting for the subway at seven in the morning in Rockefeller Center station," he said, trying to sound very knowledgeable.

"Believe me," I answered, "it will never be worse than having to deal with you every single day."

What the heck, I was leaving.

I thought I'd never hear again of my hellish boss, but for me life is always full of surprises, as you know by now. Years later, as I was about to start a day of work at *The Wall Street Journal*, someone called asking for a reference about him. I couldn't believe it. Usually, people request a reference about someone whose work you have supervised, but never about a boss.

The lady who was calling had to decide whether to hire him as the spokesperson for an important academic institution, and she explained that people skills were of the essence in that position. "We understand you have a history with him," she said, rather mysteriously. "We have heard that he sometimes, you know, breaks into– these fits. "

For a moment, I felt like taking revenge and telling that lady the whole story of my suffering under that jerk's hooves, but I chose to recuse myself and leave the conversation at that. After all, what did I care if he went on demeaning and mistreating people the world over? I was safely away from him now, and in America what's not your business is definitely not your business.

That said, I forgot to tell you the most important thing about my boss from hell: Despite the fact he always kicked me around mercilessly, I have only him to thank for the first managerial job I had in my life.

I have no clue why he gave me a promotion. Perhaps he just wanted to hold me more firmly in his grip —or even torture me more by making bigger demands on me. With him, anything was possible. But the truth is that job became the first step in the ladder that later took me to ever higher positions.

Nevertheless, I must admit that as soon as I started organizing other people's work I began to realize how difficult it is to wield even some minimal degree of power over other human beings. Some are truly nice, welcome your advice, and are quite happy to learn from you. After a while, they make useful contributions to any operation. But others curse you in their minds every single day and only think of taking your place when the time comes. What can we can we do about it? It's human nature, I guess.

However, even if I'm human, I've never gone into sudden fits of rage for no apparent reason, nor have I showered any of my workers with insults, no matter how much I felt they deserved it. Come to think of it, I have never hit my head on purpose against the walls of the offices I've occupied so far either.

It must be that I'm good-natured, after all.

There's always a Good Samaritan

THEY ARE ALWAYS THERE, when you most need them - the Good Samaritans we find on our way as we take our baby steps in this country. There aren't many, and I sure hope there were more.

As newcomers, we had but the clothes we wore. I'm not kidding. Some relatives, and even strangers, provided us with shoes and other stuff, but we had to find all the rest on our own. My wife and I worked hard, but in the beginning it always seemed that we were lacking something. It could be a TV set, a blender or some basic piece of kitchenware, if not a spare part for a car that suddenly broke down. It seemed we always needed something very urgently, and the worst part –there was never enough money to buy it. Besides, we had to eat.

I'll never forget when we first got to Ohio. A small bed my mom had bought for us, as well as a set of folding chairs and a picnic table, were all the furniture we had. The rest of our stuff we kept in a bunch of cardboard boxes and suitcases. One day, my boss came to visit, and when he saw our scarce belongings, he said confidentially: "You need to speak with Manín."

I didn't understand what he meant at first. Manín was kind of a colorful fixture in our office. He was always joking, and in his spare time he took to fix the very old cars he usually drove. He was always rubbing his hands with cream, to protect them from the cold weather. For some reason, he didn't strike me as the kind of person you would turn to if you had a furniture deficit problem.

Big mistake. The minute I told him I didn't have a penny and needed some decent furniture, Manín told me to pay him a visit at home.

"Take whatever you want," he said when I arrived, opening the door to his garage.

I couldn't believe it. There were no cars that I could see. That garage was a veritable treasure trove of all sorts of artifacts and used furniture. There was nearly everything there, from portable radios and toasters to sofas and stuffed animals. I moved awkwardly between the towering lines of curious objects, looking for what I needed. The place was like an old attic, straight out of a Hitchcock movie.

A big screen TV caught my attention. It was stuck between two refrigerators. I asked Manín if it was a color TV, and he said it was. Then, he explained he had found it in some backyard, like many of the things he kept there.

"People are just too wasteful here," he told me. "Sometimes all that's needed is a little fixing."

After a couple of hours, I took a bunch of things with me. Manín himself helped me put them on the car. They were heavy.

Later on, my boss told me Manín was in the habit of digging up in other people's trash. He was always looking for useful discards. He started doing that when he was a newcomer himself, and needed almost everything. Then, it became second nature to him, and he started helping out other new arrivals by providing them with old furniture or appliances.

"He's a little crazy," my boss concluded.

I will never be able to thank Manín enough for all his help. He came to my rescue several times when my old car left me stranded in the snow, and he also gave me other appliances later on. Besides being a part time philanthropist, Manín was an excellent mechanic.

Unfortunately, I have no idea where Manín lives now. Someone told me once he had sold his house and moved to Miami, after his wife passed away. I wouldn't be surprised; he hated cold weather. He must be older now, and of course, most likely retired. But wherever he is, I'd like to think he's still crazy enough to lend a helping hand to others all the time.

When cops knock on your door

THEY CAME EARLY. I almost didn't bother opening the door. Members of some religious group or another were in the habit of waking me up every Saturday morning to inform me the end of the world was near. But I was wrong: This time, they weren't there in the name God but that of Caesar.

The two plainclothes cops courteously identified themselves and stood at what seemed a prudent distance from me, eying me with visible suspicion. Their plastic ID's hung very obviously from their necks. They had guns I could see, too.

"You acquainted with a Dionisio Arismendi?" One of them asked me in Spanish.

"Not really," I answered, having become suspicious myself by then.

Both cops crossed looks of complicity this time.

"How strange," the other cop said in Spanish, but with a heavy English accent. "According to him, he lives here."

I began to worry. At that time of day, I wasn't ready for a grilling. Besides, while I was still a newcomer, a friend had told me to be cautious with cops. "They'll have you for breakfast," he warned.

So I put on my happy face and explained I had bought that home a year before, and only my wife, my mom and I lived there.

"I have no idea who that Arismendi fellow is," I told them, ready to close the door.

But both cops undoubtedly guessed what I was about to do.

"May we come in?" One of them asked.

I didn't answer, but I reacted as swiftly as a pit bull. I stepped out, quickly closed the door behind me, and crossed my arms firmly, as a stern guardian at my home's threshold.

"Look," I said, "I own this home and I assure you no Arismendi has ever lived here with us."

One of the cops set his hand softly on the weapon he kept, partly concealed, under his armpit. The other one stood by, stiffly.

"Is there anything else I can do for you gentlemen?" I asked.

They both exchanged glances again, but they were calm by now. It was clear to them I had no intention of engaging in a shootout. After all, this was not an episode of *Miami Vice*.

"Sorry to bother you, sir," one of the cops said. Then, they walked away sheepishly, probably harboring the feeling that I was hiding something from them. Cops get paid to be suspicious, among other things.

Every once in a while, I still ask myself who could that guy Arismendi have been, or what reasons he had to offer my address as his place of residence. Could he have been a serial killer, a drug kingpin? Who knows?

Life is full of mysteries, but I'm pretty sure of one thing: I did very well in behaving as I did. After all, I was living in the United States and not in my country of origin, where the police would have kicked the door in and put me away in some cold dungeon until I confessed I was Arismendi's brother-in-law, a clever CIA operative or something worse.

Lessons often come with a beating, according to a Spanish proverb. And civics lessons are sometimes learned very much the hard way, too. In America, an honest citizen's home is like his castle. Fortunately, the cops have never knocked on my door again. Maybe they learned their lesson, too.

Beware of success

WANT A GOOD PIECE OF ADVICE? Watch out for envious people. They are everywhere, just like God, and if you think you won't find them in America, you are very wrong.

As a newcomer, I thought I would be free of that plague here. In this country, you have a reasonable expectation of reaching certain goals. After some time, by putting your mind and your will to work, and above all, with the patience of the credit cards and the banks, you can jump financial brackets, buy a small home and even drive a brand new car once in a while. Hey, I'm no Donald Trump and I can't complain.

Why should we covet someone else's success when we can quietly pursue our own?

But envious people don't believe in the fruits of hard work, because they secretly kneel at the altar of the goddess Fortune. For them, life is like a rigged lottery, where they always get stuck with a losing ticket. People like you and I probably have the help of some powerful cousin, if we're not benefiting from a dark pact with the Devil. Otherwise, how can we account for our blessings?

Appearances can be deceitful, though. The envious aren't always so obvious. Sometimes they pretend to be your buddies. They break into a smile when they see you, shake your hand and may even embrace you warmly; but they actually want to see you bound to a wheelchair and begging for money in the streets.

Not long ago, I bumped into one of these types, a very talented writer who had always refused to promote his work or earn a living based on his skills, because he firmly believed geniuses live in obscurity and die penniless. For many years, he worked as a forklift operator in a construction warehouse. He thought it was an excellent training for a future Nobel Prize.

"So, how's it going?" He asked, after a while.

When I told him I was living comfortably in another city, running a new publication in Spanish, he frowned.

"Too bad," he said finally. "You're always looking for excuses not to write.".

I suppose it was his peculiar way of recriminating me for "selling out" and avoiding the pecuniary sacrifices that, according to his version of life, inevitably come with a talent for words.

I didn't want to tell him I wrote all the time, and that different from him, I got paid for it. Why tell him, besides, about the many sacrifices, big and small, that attaining any measure of success involves? In short, why make him more depressed than he already was?

So I shrugged and treated him to a cup of Cuban coffee. I've never seen him again.

More recently, another so-called friend, an artist whose paintings could sell for thousands of dollars, but who chose to become a part-time nurse's assistant almost the minute he set foot in America, sent me an email, accusing me of doing something I've never done in my life: giving myself airs. "Who are you pretending to be exactly?" He asked sarcastically in his brief note.

I answered him as ruthlessly as he deserved. After rhetorically lamenting the long nights he had to spend at the hospital, and how little he got paid for it, I asked him quietly not to blame me for his dark fate. "You certainly have worked hard for it," I told him. I was very glad he never answered. My electronic mailbox is a total disaster.

What else can I say?

After growing old and wiser in this country, I'm pretty sure I've heard it all. Believe me, for some, to succeed is almost sinful. So if you end up doing reasonably well, don't be surprised if rumors begin to spread about your hidden links to drug trafficking or the government secrets you sold for a fortune. Losers lack almost everything, except a great imagination.

Don't even think of getting sick

IF YOU THINK LIFE is expensive in America, just wait till you end up in a hospital here. If acute appendicitis doesn't kill you, you may well die of a heart attack when you take a look at the bill.

As a newcomer, people warned me not to get sick. I thought they were concerned about my health, but years later I realized they were actually worried about my bank account.

One morning, I woke up with a sharp pain at the very center of my belly. It wouldn't go away. Could I have been poisoned with the pizza I ate the night before? My wife drove me quickly to the hospital. To our relief, it turned out to be my gall bladder. It was swollen and necrotic.

"You need surgery," the doctor said.

I was livid. Some people literally love to visit doctors all the time and always seem to have an active reservation for the operating room. I, on the contrary, have always been allergic to scalpels. But I had no choice this time. The doctor insisted if they didn't operate, the infection would move to my pancreas and I would die in horrible pain.

I was immediately admitted, and once tucked in bed, I was connected to a bunch of gadgets that measured one and each of my vital signs. They beeped from time to time, then they would remain silent for a while, only to start beeping again later.

All sorts of specialists came to visit me, even at the most unseemly hours. They took my pulse, checked my blood pressure, asked about allergies and made me sign long documents I didn't quite understand.

A nurse came in next morning. She brought a pair of elastic socks and made me put them on. They were as tight as tourniquets. According to her, they would prevent blood clots from forming in my legs, which could kill me or leave me paralyzed. Back where I came from, I had never heard of such a thing, but it made me very scared and I obediently followed her instructions.

Another day, a small, thin man appeared out of nowhere, bringing a weird contraption with him. It was a plastic box connected to a tube. He explained patiently how I would need to blow through the tube. Every time I did that, a ping-pong ball would go up and down inside the box. This simple exercise was supposed to prevent me from developing a hernia after surgery. How ridiculous, I thought.

Not thinking twice, I told that gentleman to go away. He did, but not before I signed a long document releasing him from all and any liability.

I was a nervous wreck by the time I went under the knife. The previous days I had felt like a death row inmate, counting every single second to surgery; but I went through the procedure like a breeze. When I woke up, I had a six-inch scar at the top of my stomach.

Some time later, the bills started pouring in, many of them –and all conveying serious warnings in case I didn't pay up. Apparently, quite a bunch of people had something to gain from my gall bladder removal: the surgeon, the hospital, the anesthesiologists, the radiologists and a legion of assistants. The price for some little pills ran up to $30. Even with insurance, I ended up paying thousands.

That said, I had the pleasure of refusing to pay for the ping-pong box I never used. They had put it in the bill by mistake. Out of curiosity, I looked the price up –it was about $500! What a toy...

Soft tissues and fender-benders

ONE DAY, I HAD AN ACCIDENT. I mean someone's car bumped into mine, not the other way around.

I was coming out of the parking lot of a building in Miami when I felt something hit the right side of my car. Not very hard, but it made my Mazda 326 shudder lightly. Right there, I stopped and turned the engine off.

A young guy jumped out of a sports car waving his hands in my face and asking me if I was blind. I told him I wasn't, and reminded him he was the one who had rammed my vehicle. He insisted, excitedly, that I was to blame. Why argue with him?

I took a look at the damages –a mere dent on the passenger side door- and then sat quietly on the curb, waiting for the police to show up. It was my first car accident and, quite naturally, I was full of emotions. As a newcomer, ten years before, no one had explained what to do in a situation like this. It was what they would call now a "learning experience".

Then, a patrol car appeared out of nowhere. The young guy ran up to the cop, telling him how I had almost cut his life short, and what a danger I posed for law-abiding drivers like him.

I didn't say a word. It's the best thing you can do when dealing with cops. So I handed the officer my documents and waited patiently as he wrote up a report and made a sketch of our pathetic little fender-bender. When he was done, the cop gave us each copies of the report. The young guy was on the verge of tears.

"But it doesn't say here whose fault it was!" He whined.

The cop smiled.

"In this life, everyone's a little at fault, sir," he explained, rather philosophically.

A couple days later, as I looked through our correspondence at home, I noticed a curious envelope. It was kind of long, white and had a classy letterhead on it. When I opened it, I was totally shocked.

It was a letter from an attorney, saying his client had been injured in a crash with my car, and urging me to report the accident as soon as possible. What was that supposed to mean? Could it be the opening salvo in a legal battle in which I would lose my life's savings? Last time I looked, that young punk was in very good health. What had happened since then?

I had never needed a lawyer before, but I had a friend who was a good one. So I drove to his office to show him the ominous letter. He took a quick look at it, shrugged and threw it aside, as if it was a piece of trash.

"Relax, Manny," he said. I was fuming.

"But it's a total lie!" I protested. "I saw him walk away on his own two legs!"

My friend reflected for a moment. He then said that some injuries don't show any symptoms until a day after the accident.

"They're soft tissue injuries and they can be very painful," he explained. I was outraged. How could he give any credence to that kind of BS?

My attorney friend forgot all about me. He gave some quick instructions to his secretary, and he was signing a letter of his own in a matter of minutes.

"What are you telling them?" I asked, with much concern.

"Don't worry," my friend said, tucking the letter in a long, white envelope with his own fancy letterhead.

I never heard from the young man or his shyster again. And by the way, I never had another car accident either. But I remained curious about what my lawyer friend had written in his letter.

Years later, in one of many visits to Miami, I ran into my friend in a local Spanish restaurant. After saying hello, I thanked him again for his help in my only traffic accident. Out of curiosity, I insisted he tell me what he wrote in his letter. I assumed it was strongly worded, since it seemed to have solved all my legal problems for good. My friend burst in laughter.

"I told them you were injured, too, Manny," he answered. "Seriously injured."

Ignorance comes at a high price

WITH ALL THE TALK ABOUT ENGLISH ONLY, some people are apparently going nuts.

While some believe it should be mandatory for everyone to be born with English-language skills, others are bent on having their host country adopt their mother tongue as a matter of law.

How foolish.

I already spoke English fluently when I came to America. But not all immigrants are so fortunate.

For a time, my wife had to use sign language to buy things in stores, and even pretend she understood all our neighbors said to her. Later on, with good teachers and the help of the TV programs she liked, she learned enough English to get by.

It strikes me as funny, however, that instead of taking the trouble of learning English, some immigrants hold on to their ignorance of the language as a badge of honor. A gentleman whose acquaintance I made in my first place of work in America comes to my mind. He nearly went into a fit when he found out that I, a mere newcomer, could speak so freely with all the Gringos around us.

"I've been living for 20 years in this country and I don't speak a word of English!!" He boasted during a lunch break in the cafeteria. "My son takes care of any emergency."

Poor children. From a tender age, they find themselves taking care of their parents' "emergencies", as if they were the adults. Can you imagine a ten-year-old girl acting as an interpreter in the purchase of a home or car, or translating for her mom in a doctor's visit? That's horrible. It smacks of child abuse.

I'm certainly no fan of accelerated assimilation. Nothing ticks me off so much as those Latinos who, barely a few months after arriving in this country, begin to use that dumb dialect called "Spanglish". They change their names to Frank, Sam, Chuck or Ralph, thinking this will make them sound "more American". Poor devils. They don't learn English, but they pervert the only language they really know. And when they don't understand what's been said to them, they go into their favorite mantra, *"Me-nospeak-eenglich, me-nospeak-eenglich."*

Never mind English Only. No one can force you to learn anything, but the truth is, in America, if you don't speak English you're basically screwed. I know of highly educated professionals, even some physicians and a couple of talented writers, who are doomed to the lowest of jobs only because they don't speak English —or because they learned the wrong language.

A Cuban lady I know devoted many years to learning French. Back in Havana, she attended classes twice a week and her pronunciation in that language was absolutely charming. I loved to listen to her reciting Baudelaire. I used to tease her about it: "Talk to me in French, baby!" I always thought she'd move to Paris if she ever left the country, but that didn't happen. Instead of moving close to the Champs Elysées, she's now renting an apartment in Miami's Little Havana. How ironic. Very few people speak French there, I'm sure.

Never mind the bigots. English is like the Latin of modern times. It's the common tongue for trade and international relations. You either speak it or want to speak it.

Can you imagine living in Classical Antiquity and being unable to talk and interact with the Romans? You'd end up as a slave in a salt mine, or worse, as a circus gladiator. So learn, my friends. It beats fighting the lions anytime.

The day I took the oath

IT WAS A RAINY MORNING. I didn't take it as a bad omen, or as any other thing for that matter. In Florida, it rains a lot. It could have been worse, with one of those hurricanes.

After 12 years in this country, paying my taxes and abiding by its laws, it made sense to pledge allegiance to its flag, and in the process, earn the right to vote for those who rule this land.

It wasn't easy, but I had good training. As a newcomer, I was witness to a heated presidential campaign, and since then I got into the habit of placing my bets either for Republicans or Democrats. It was a difficult guessing game. That's democracy for you. There are places where the same candidate gets elected every single time. That doesn't happen in America.

I have seen several presidents come and go since I arrived in this country, and quite a number of congressmen and mayors, too. Some have been better than others, but no one expects them to be at the helm forever. All go out of fashion at some point, just like clothing and performing artists —and it's better that way. Otherwise, life would be too boring.

So I took the oath of citizenship one day in May, with a mix of excitement and good feelings. Suddenly, by raising my right hand in that auditorium, I renounced all my past national loyalties as well as any claim to nobility I could ever have. Imagine, all those dreams of becoming a count or a baron were immediately shattered by that single act.

Many congratulated me that day —my mom was first in line. But one of my best friends dampened those warm feelings when I called to break the good news to him.

"You have forsaken your homeland, your roots," he said, in a tone of voice that betrayed pious anger.

Quite frankly, I didn't expect that of him. My friend had been brought to this country as a child. It was a miracle that he still spoke some Spanish. He certainly had never lacked opportunities here, and had reached incredible heights in his professional life. He owned a beautiful home and had a wonderful family, quite deserving of the sweetest American Dream. How could he reject all of that?

I explained that, over the years, all the links to my country of origin had been vanishing and were but tenuous memories by now. This didn't mean that my native land had less of an emotional appeal for me. Of course I still held feelings for it. But if I was going make a life for myself in this country from now on, it made no sense to cling to a nationality that, for all effects, was no longer mine.

"Your homeland is where you find your happiness," I concluded bluntly.

My friend remained silent and quickly changed the subject. He made some comments about an article I had published a week before and then said goodbye, claiming he was in a hurry. I never heard from him until years later, when I came back to Miami in one of many visits.

He called me early one morning to tell me all about it. He had just become a citizen and wanted me to be the first to know.

"And why is that?" I asked, somewhat alarmed. It always scares me when somebody wants to tell me a secret.

"For the many foolish things I said that time," he answered.

"I don't even remember," I said.

It was almost true. I'm very forgetful and had no reason to recriminate him either. Becoming a citizen and singing the *Star-Spangled Banner* is like making an adoption official. What documents grant you will not exclude the entitlements that come from blood and heritage. Homeland is happiness, absolutely.

Eating your heart out

WHAT A PLEASURE IT IS to dine in a good restaurant! In this country, depending on the area where you live, you can take your pick. Since, as we are told, this is a melting pot, all cuisines are represented here.

New York is famous for its Italian, Greek and Chinese eateries. Washington, our capital, boasts of having a restaurant for every country in the world. This may sound like an exaggeration, but it's close to the truth. Miami is, doubtless, a paradise of Latin American food, from Cuban and Colombian dishes to those of Nicaragua, Peru, Mexico and Argentina. Ah, just to think about it makes my mouth water... That's probably why I became a restaurant critic later on.

But as a newcomer, I couldn't afford to engage in these flavorful adventures —nor in any other sort of adventures, by the way. We had to do with what we were able to buy in the market every week. With that, and maybe an occasional visit to La Carreta in Calle Ocho. We were poor. What else could we do?

Then, one time, a friend recommended Yayo's. I thought he was kidding, since he knew quite well how squalid my pockets were. I had never heard about that place and thought it was just one of those classy joints where a plate of rice and beans can cost you a week's salary, only because they've given it a French name or something. But I was wrong.

Yayo's was a modest but clean, buffet-type restaurant, and its prices certainly did not require financing. It's been a long time and I doubt the place is even in business by now; but I remember that for a very low sum (maybe $5) you could eat all you wanted there, to your heart's content. They served everything: roast pork, steaks, chicken in a myriad ways, all colors of beans, fish, as well as mountains of rice, plantains and French fries.

"All-You-Can-Eat," they called it. I was fascinated.

The first time I went to Yayo's, I served myself shovels of roast pork, white rice and black beans for starters. When I was done with that, I returned for chicken breast, yellow rice and fried ripe plantains. Then, I dealt with a baked fish filet and a huge portion of mashed potatoes. At the very end, I was ready for the desserts: bread and rice puddings, flan... I had to loosen my belt by that time. My head was spinning.

"Are you OK?" Someone asked.

It was one of the waiters, who had realized I was in a quasi-catatonic state.

"More or less," I said.

He turned around and came back with a glass of cold water.

"You're not from here, are you?" He asked.

"I came from Cuba months ago," I told him, between gulps of water.

"I can tell," he said.

"Why?"

"The way you eat," he answered, smiling.

He was very right. My hunger was ancient, irrational, the combined voracity of all of the Third World —and then more. Faced with a never-ending source of nourishment, I could not find a way to placate it. If I kept eating like that, someone would have to call an ambulance, so I decided to call it quits. But I was still puzzled about something.

"Is this a good business for you guys?" I asked.

"Of course, plenty of customers," the waiter said.

I could see that. Dozens of people were circling the buffet at that very moment, and picking at everything.

"They are so many," I insisted. "What if you run out of food?"

The waiter laughed.

"Not all of them share your appetite," he said.

He probably meant that as a compliment. I don't know. I still wonder. Then I left, burping happily on the way out.

Lose that moustache

YOU'RE EXPECTED TO MAKE some critical decisions in your life. I'm not speaking of finding refuge in a Tibetan monastery or of suddenly adopting a strict vegetarian diet, certainly nothing so drastic. It's about something as mundane as growing a moustache, an act with which I celebrated my coming of age, shortly after I was 20 years old.

This thing about coming of age is, of course, just a figure of speech, since my insistence in engaging in this ungrateful line of work —writing- probably qualifies me as pretty immature. Nevertheless, I was quite convinced that moustache gave me not only a distinguished appearance but —above all- that air of wisdom that eluded me so much at the time.

It wasn't one of those pencil-thin moustaches, the kind you have to trim every morning. Mine was rather wild, natural, and rebellious. Its tips rolled upward in a funny curl, like the moustaches on those stereotypical Mexicans you see in the movies. I thought of it as very elegant.

But as a newcomer in this country, a good friend of mine advised me to get rid of it.

"That moustache sucks," he told me, bluntly.

I couldn't believe it. That cute shadow of hair had been with me for so many years, the mere idea of killing it with a single blow appeared to be almost criminal to me. My friend insisted no one would give me a job looking like that, adding that moustaches had gone out of fashion long ago, just like miniskirts.

Could this be possible? I asked myself. Until then, I had assumed this country was a beacon of freedom, where everything, from long hair and sideburns to naked midriffs and legs were accepted, no questions asked. You could even curse the President publicly —as long as you paid your taxes, of course. It seemed I had been under the wrong impression. Anyway, I made a last attempt to defend my view.

"Burt Reynolds has a moustache," I argued.

"Yes," my friend said, "but you're no Burt Reynolds."

Who could argue with that?

This appeared to seal my moustache's fate. Besides my friend, all agreed I should lose it —my wife, my aunt, my cousins, and even my mom. They insisted I looked ugly, dirty, and worst of all, very, very old. What can I say? These were strong arguments, too.

So I waited a few days, and one morning, after crossing myself, I slowly began to shave: First, the bristles on my cheeks and chin; then, the scant hair on my neck. After that, with the same momentum, I went for the hair on my upper lip. The warm water and shaving cream made the operation go smoother. In a matter of minutes, my moustache was gone.

It was mentally painful, but I must admit that as soon as I looked at my face in the mirror, I noticed the difference. My reflection was clean, youthful —even trustworthy, I might add. I wasn't sure this would help me get a job anytime soon, but doubtless it was a good start.

You gain many things when you come to America —excellent professional opportunities, freedom, and especially the right to decide your own fate. But in leaving your native land behind, you're deprived of other things you appreciate: old friendships, family memories, as well as the streets and places that nurtured your soul as you grew up.

It's the inevitable give and take in which we all engage when we pack up our stuff and embark on that last trip abroad. There's plenty of reason to rejoice, but there's a sad part to this voyage, too. I, for example, lost my moustache. Not a big deal, I think. It could have been worse.

Why I'm not scared of Friday the 13th

FRIDAY THE 13TH IS a fateful occasion in America. It's the ideal day to travel by plane, because there are plenty of tickets available. You can easily rent a place for a party and make reservations in a restaurant, too. No one wants to sign contracts, and many employees call in sick on a day like that.

In these incredulous times, very few people can afford to be superstitious, of course, but why run the risk? As they say back where I came from, "Better prevent than to lament."

Fortunately, I didn't arrive in this country on a Friday the 13th; but I learned of this old American tradition in the best possible way: in the movies.

At that time, they were showing the first part of *Friday the 13th* and the evil of that day was revealed to me the minute I began to watch the carnage produced on the screen by the monster Jason.

In case you don't remember, Jason, with his cracked hockey mask, was the main character in that film and all of its sequels, in which he, the most irrational, ruthless and resilient of all murderers, ended with strong blows of his machete the lives of his victims –foolish, lustful teenagers, all apparently engaged in a permanent summer vacation.

I've never been unfortunate enough to cross ways with Jason in all these years, nor with any other serial killer, for that matter. As a newcomer, I was just too busy making an honest living in this country. Nothing bad has ever happened to me on a Friday the 13th either, and for a very good reason: I'm not a Gringo.

Back where I came from (as in many other countries, I suppose), we know too well what the true day for bad luck is. We don't fall for cheap superstitions. Anyone in his right mind knows that the day you shouldn't go to work, sign a contract or even turn your car's engine on is *Tuesday* the 13th, and not Friday, as many wrongly believe here.

As they say back where I came from, "Do not marry or take a trip on Tuesday the 13th." The rhyme was lost in translation, I'm sorry.

Over time, all the poor devils who have dared to violate this sacred rule have found themselves involved in horrible traffic accidents, or have seen their lives shattered after saying "I do" to the ladies of their dreams on such an ominous date.

As much as I've investigated, I don't know where the Gringos got the idea that Friday the 13th is the day for bad luck –probably from one of those calendars that some ill-advised farmers compile every year. They're wrong all the time, warning us of rain and hale when a spell of sunny weather is on its way, or predicting a bountiful corn harvest when only bananas look like a good investment. With so many wise Latino psychics around, how can you even pay attention to all that garbage?

That said, to be fair, Americans do deserve some credit, OK? After all, they invented lots of useful stuff, like the vacuum cleaner and the electric bulb. And apparently they also got right the day of the month on which we should not venture in the streets, go to work, or even fall in love. It's the 13th, a fatidic number on which all of us can at least agree.

Better the birds in the sky than the one you have at hand

APPARENTLY, RUNNING AWAY runs in my family.

A distant relative of mine on my mother's side, Cirilo Villaverde, escaped from jail in mid-19th century Cuba. He ended up in New York, where he married a wealthy lady and went on to publish the first Cuban novel, *Cecilia Valdés*.

Joseíto, one of my grand uncles, vanished in Havana, circa 1905. After a time, the family assumed the worst, and even held a funeral for him *in absentia*. But a decade later, he came back from the dead at the door of his former home, wearing the uniform of the U.S. Army and speaking in some kind of broken Spanish no one understood. His name was now Joe López and he lived in Baltimore.

Mauricio, my grandfather on my father's side, was barely 13 years old when he joined the Cuban independence army. Since he didn't know how to use a gun, he was assigned horse-grooming duties. What a task that must have been! Maybe that's the reason he didn't think twice when later on some American soldiers fighting the Spanish-American war suggested he move up north, to Atlanta, where he learned English and finished high school.

Life can be very strange. Who can argue with that?

I often ask myself what compelled these three men to leave everything behind, to abandon an environment full of friends, relatives and familiar places, only to submerge themselves in a strange and often hostile world where they could certainly prevail, but where they could as easily end up begging for money in street corners —and in a foreign language, too.

I can understand very well why my novelist relative fled Cuba. Quite frankly, the choice is clear between a colonial Spanish prison and the bustling streets of Manhattan. But my grand uncle was no political prisoner, much less a conspirator. He was barely a child when he jumped on a foreign ship in the port of Havana, destination unknown. And as far as I know, my grandfather Mauricio was a practical, conservative man, not very prone to succumb to dreams or fantasies. After some time, he returned to his hometown of Camagüey and never contemplated a life abroad again.

The truth is, you have to be a bit *loco* to become an immigrant. *Loco* or desperate, which is almost the same. It runs contrary to the most basic common sense, and to that Spanish proverb: "Better a single bird in your hand than a hundred in the sky."

Why would you forsake the safety you enjoy at home to pursue a dream Don Quixote himself would not follow? Why jump on a boat or cross a treacherous river not knowing exactly what you will find on the other side?

As a newcomer, I was so *loco* or desperate it never crossed my mind that, in running away, I was following an old family tradition —a tradition of madness I would not wish on anyone else, come to think of it.

I write all this now, with the quiet relief of someone who has finally reached a safe harbor, as well as with the wisdom of one who has survived to tell his frightful story.

Because in coming here, my friends, we all placed our bets on the birds up in the sky, and not on the one we held close and comfortably in our hand. We have either become filthy rich or remained poor like rats, but every time we gaze up at a cloud, we feel an irrepressible need to trap it.

Time to go home?

THEY SAY YOU DON'T know how American you've become until you go on your first trip back "home".

I've never embarked on that voyage, not in my wildest fantasies. As a newcomer in America, I promised myself not to. They made it so difficult for us to come here, I can't imagine ever going back. So every time I get the chance, I jump on a plane and take off for somewhere, anywhere, but that place I used to call home. It's my sweet revenge.

I've traveled a lot by now —South America, Mexico, the Caribbean, Europe. To step on a firm, big chunk of land is the dream of every insular creature like me, and I've enjoyed it to the fullest. Spain is my favorite destination, even if I'm not a part of the castanets-and-tambourines crowd.

"Where are you from?" I am asked often in hotels and airports the world over, after someone sees the eagle in the cover of my passport. When I answer I'm an American, they eye me with suspicion. They probably think I'm lying, or at best, pulling their legs.

"Yes, but from where?" They insist sometimes, curious about that hidden, now abandoned nationality of mine. I'm betrayed, perhaps, by the fact I'm not tall, blond and blue-eyed.

It seems not all are ready to acknowledge a citizen of the Latin American diaspora –a living, walking statistic; one of the many who come here every day on a boat, by plane, even swimming. Those, in sum, who have embraced America, and are now called Hispanics or Latinos, as if we all came from the same country.

Sometimes, just for fun, I ask them to take a guess. I've already been mistaken for Venezuelan, Colombian, Puerto Rican, Guatemalan, Arab –even Greek! My old Cuban accent must have become terrible by now.

By the way, I have a Peruvian buddy who's the object of many jokes each time he visits his family in Lima. All his neighbors tell him he speaks just like a character from *La Tremenda Corte,* an old radio comedy show, originally produced in Havana but still very popular in South America. I'm not surprised. My friend has been living all these years in Miami. What other accent could he acquire? He sounds absolutely Cuban!

As for my accent, I must admit that over the years, it has been feeding on perhaps too many voices, from the typical Dominican "sing-song" to the gravity of certain syllables in Venezuelan dialect. My vocabulary has become an eclectic mixture of different slang and expressions, all absorbed from Mexican, Chilean, Spanish and Puerto Rican colleagues. I find myself at times using words imported from many countries, except the one I came from.

After all this time, I don't really know what I am, or what I say. *Ay, bendito.* I'm like a salad. I don't know if I was born in Havana, Tijuana, Bogota, San Juan or God knows where. I love roast pork, but also the sweet *tres leches* and tacos, too, and I won't eat my beef without soaking it in *chimuchurri* sauce. I've lost my accent, my mannerisms and most likely my soul, but I don't miss them, honestly.

Life is beautiful where I am now.

♥ New York? Better think about it

MOST OF THOSE WHO dream of coming to America usually imagine this country as some sort of big New York, or better still, a huge version of Manhattan where tall buildings touch the clouds and there are myriads of theaters, discos and other urban charms. I don't know; maybe they've seen too many movies.

As a newcomer, I, too, entertained such fantasies, but they all vanished after a while, pushed aside by the stubborn, mundane realities of the many places where we have lived and worked. In any event, one fine day we ended up living in the Big Apple, and this is the story of my disappointment.

I don't mean to spoil any of your dreams, but if you're contemplating a move to that megalopolis so many people claim to love, you're in for very big surprise.

For starters, you can kiss your car goodbye. New Yorkers hate cars, for the simple reason they have no use for them. The streets of Manhattan are narrow and labyrinthine, and full of those yellow vehicles called taxis, whose drivers are sworn to squash any human being, animal or artifact they may find on the way to their destinations. You'd have to be mad to challenge them.

And then, if you succeed in keeping safe from these road warriors, you will find it very difficult to park your car anywhere without paying the city an extraordinary tribute, sometimes in the order of $30 per hour, or even more. Better hire a limousine, like Thalía or Ricky Martin do. It's cheaper —and classier, too.

You can also forget about living in a large, clean home where your children can run around, and where you can enjoy some rest after a day's work. Space is mightier than gold in the Big Apple, its prices quite deserving of that quintessential New Yorker, Donald Trump.

A simple studio (or efficiency, as some would call it elsewhere in this country) can cost you more than a $1,000 a month, rats and cockroaches included, as well as the dubious privilege of going up long stairs to reach your humble residence. Don't even think of buying there either —no mortgage could finance those prices, not with your salary anyway.

Some say you make more money "up north", and that may be true —up to a certain point. Salaries are higher than in other, less illustrious areas, but after all the deductions, including those of the state, the city itself, and even some weird tax to provide health care to indigent patients, you end up as poor as you were before.

And, of course, I forgot to tell you about the cold weather; that ruthless chill that digs deep into your gut and even your soul, joined most of the time by plenty of that white dust called snow. If you have ever dreamed of witnessing first hand this wonder of Nature, try shoveling it before or after a day's work. Let me tell you, you will need no further exercise to keep fit.

Not to contradict Frank Sinatra, folks, but before you pack up and start singing *New York, New York,* I would suggest you think it over.

If you don't like the place where you live now, there are plenty of other warmer, cheaper, friendlier and more comfortable choices. Take it from me. I now live in Florida.

That Christmas spirit

MY FIRST CHRISTMAS HERE was serious business. No, I didn't spend my holidays in the hospital, and Santa didn't punish me with a bag of coal stones either.

As a newcomer in America, I was only partly aware of what I was getting into. Christmas here is a very solemn occasion, but it has a very strong commercial component as well. That's not necessarily bad; lots of people are buying presents, and merchants have to make a living too. So, as soon as December showed up in my 1980 calendar, I prepared my squalid pockets for the worst.

I made a list as small as my family, and after some quick calculations, I concluded I would survive that joyous season. Putting some little presents under our Christmas tree wasn't going to break my piggy bank. With the little savings we had, I figured I was well prepared.

What I didn't expect was the treacherous attack of an old American tradition —exchanging presents at the office party. You know, that habit of holding a drawing in which you always end up giving a gift to your worst enemy —and he to you. What for? Sometimes you take all that hate to your grave, Christmas or no Christmas.

I wasn't concerned at first. All my co-workers knew I was as poor as a refugee, so I thought any modest gift would do. If need be, I could skip next month's phone bill, or borrow some money from my mom, who fortunately, had a terrible memory.

That was that until I picked my little piece of folded paper in the drawing. Everyone applauded, but my hands began to shake immediately. With my luck, I had picked none other than the newspaper's editor, a middle-aged gentleman with a taste for what some would call the finer things in life. He drove a Mercedes, loved cognac and cigars, and only wore tailored suits.

"Don't worry, he will understand," the girls in the office told me, compassionately.

But the mere notion of giving that guy an old tie or a bottle of seasoning powder as a Christmas gift made me very jittery. On top of it, the only tie I owned at the time –and which I could pass on to him- was actually a hand-me-down, with loose threads already showing on one of its edges. It was unthinkable to disguise it as a present.

Days later, I paid a visit to a very exclusive department store. My mother had extended me one of her many long-term loans, and I was looking for something that was neither costly nor miserable, just in between. That is to say something nearly impossible to find, if you know what I mean.

Finally, after looking around for quite a while, I discovered a smallish bottle of men's perfume in one of the stands. Brand name, as he liked things to be –and with a 10 percent discount! These were the most reluctant 45 bucks I've paid in my whole life, but at least I would be able to attend the gift exchange ceremony with some measure of dignity.

The editor was delighted. He didn't wait to open the package, and when he saw the tiny bottle of expensive perfume, he embraced me and thanked me profusely many times. As for myself, I didn't dare to open his gift, being very sure it was something exquisite, quite deserving of the editor's good taste.

I was so wrong.

The minute I got home, still glowing with that generous Christmas aura, I sat on the sofa and opened the package, which had a beautiful red ribbon on top of it. Inside, buried in lots of soft, colorful tissues, I found my gift –a non-descript tie, brand unknown, with the obvious scent of old age, and, of course, with loose threads quite visible on one of its edges.

Pay up after the champagne

WHILE MANY RUSH to celebrate the coming of a new year, I start thinking about the next. It's not some kind of panic attack; it's not that I'm feeling too optimistic either. Heck, the pages in the calendar are going to turn anyway, no matter what. In any case, I'm going to become older and grumpier.

The coming of a New Year is not necessarily a harbinger of better things, nor of important changes in your career, or of a quick turn of your emotions, as some astrologers would want you to believe. It's actually a rather mundane occasion in this country –the moment you inevitably must sit down and spill your financial guts to Uncle Sam. In other words, between January and April, you will have to do your taxes.

As a newcomer, most of the people I knew avoided talking to me about this thorny subject. My very eloquent cousin never explained that each year brings with it that difficult season in which we open our ledgers –and sometimes even our hearts- to the suspicious eyes of the government. We must make calculations, state clearly what we earned and what we spent; add, subtract, multiply and divide. And pay, of course, if you owe something.

"This is Communism —only with food," a distraught Cuban friend said, after he learned he would have to cough up more than $200.

The truth is my friend had come to America ten years before and the small business he ran was thriving. I think he was in real estate or something. He drove a brand new car and was always dressed up. I, on the other hand, had very little to declare that January of 1981 —barely minimum wage for a family of three. Can you imagine? Even so, just looking at the IRS form made me shiver. I've never been too good with numbers.

"Better get yourself an accountant," someone suggested.

But I simply couldn't afford it. The best accountants charged a fortune, and with the help of the worse of them, those that charge you just 5 or 10 bucks for doing your taxes on their kitchen table, you could end up in jail.

"Remember Al Capone," a neighbor warned me at the time. "They didn't get him for being a mobster, but for cheating on his taxes."

Well, I said to myself, if I'm going to go to jail, better get there on my own —and on my own kitchen table, too. So I borrowed a small calculator, found myself the simplest tax form, and armed with a pencil, I did my return in a matter of minutes. It was easier than I had thought, and it brought me a sweet surprise, too. I not only didn't owe Uncle Sam any money, but he was actually going to reimburse me $600. My friend the real estate guy was amazed. Nothing like that had ever happened to him.

"Are you sure?" He asked.

Years later, I found out the reason for such a generous deal. It was because we lived "under the poverty ceiling", as bureaucrats here say.

A lot of time has gone by since then. I haven't become rich, but my finances have improved somewhat. I can't complain. But sometimes, when I look up at the ceiling, I remember my first tax return.

The pain of buying a home

B UYING A HOUSE IS like falling in love. So learn from love, ye real estate agents. An arrow's thrust decides it all, and the romance, as you probably know, may last forever, or end up in boredom, infidelity and even divorce.

As a newcomer, the notion of buying a home was for me as remote as climbing to the top of Mount Everest. Looking at the prices, it frightened me to think how much I would need to save in order to buy my own dwelling. Later on, I realized financing was conceived to deal with such a large expense. But at the time, how could I know about that?

The truth is, one day Cupid suddenly took a shot at me. I had driven to a housing community in the outskirts of Miami to sign the lease for a small duplex we were going to rent elsewhere, and then I saw it, tucked in the folds of a *cul-de-sac*. It was a cutie, with French doors and a small garden. After that, I took my wife to see it, and she fell in love with it, too. A couple days later, we were making our first offer.

But this story isn't about that love, but rather about the wedding. That is, the anguish and the travails of paying the required dowry for that lovely bride.

Don't fool yourself. Buying a home, especially your first one, is like having your teeth pulled out without the benefit of anesthesia. Fortunately, on that painful journey, I had the company of a good attorney, and not only good but excellent. He could calculate your 30-year mortgage as easily as a tip for a waiter. I wonder where he is right now.

Almost from the beginning, he told me, pessimistically: "Manny, in this transaction you're the most helpless; that's why you need me." And he was very right. Everyone involved in that sale seemed bent on having us buy that house, no matter the costs or the conditions: two realtors, the mortgage broker, the bank and God know how many other parties.

They set up all sorts of traps for us, from blank spaces in the contract forms to offers of costly and unnecessary services. But my lawyer detected all their schemes, crossed out the blank spaces and rejected all their tricks with a quick phone call to one office or another. My wife and I were outraged. We wanted to back away, but my attorney just smiled calmly.

"Easy, Manny, it's just part of the game," he said.

We couldn't bring ourselves to believe that one of the realtors, outwardly a friend of ours, would try to deceive us, but obviously all is fair in war and business.

Finally, just when we were about to close on the deal, a contractor who was helping us with the inspections determined the house had some structural damage. The sellers had not shared this minor detail, but the costs of fixing it would run in the thousands of dollars. We thought the purchase was doomed, but my attorney solved this impasse by giving the sellers a simple ultimatum: either you pay for the repairs or the deal is off.

It was a quick remedy, because the sellers paid, taking the money from the realtors' commission, and we finally bought our house. We all shook hands in an office one afternoon, smiling as if nothing had happened. Congratulations!

Years later, when we moved to New York, we sold the house at a good profit. We hired the same lawyer and the transaction took three months, but gave us very little trouble, to tell you the truth. On the contrary, we had our share of fun setting up traps of our own for the buyers, at a distance. This time, the ones to fall in love were others, and it was their turn to sit on the dentist's chair.

The mother of all diets

GOING HUNGRY CAN BE TOUGH. No question about that.

As a newcomer in this country, I thought I had put behind me all those Third World hardships, especially that feeling of emptiness you get in your belly, and that peculiar anxiety your palate suffers when your appetite remains somewhat unsatisfied.

But I was in for a big surprise again.

One time, I was quietly working on a huge Cuban sandwich in the cafeteria of my first place of work in America, when my eyes took in inadvertently what was on one of my co-worker's plate. It almost made me cry.

Emelina's lunch consisted of a very thin piece of toasted bread, neatly covered by a single leaf of lettuce. A full glass of a white liquid that tried to resemble milk stood close by. She stirred it with a spoon and took a sip.

"What's that?" I asked, horrified.

"Shut up," she said. "I'm on a diet. Please don't make this harder for me, OK?"

Emelina then started devouring that frugal lunch as if it was some delicious beef stew, or even something more substantial. Watching her made me feel so sad I couldn't finish my own lunch.

Since then, I've been fascinated by this country's obsession with dieting. The evidence shows up everywhere –in magazines, newspapers, TV shows, and even in the huge displays of self-help material you'll find in most bookstores.

There are all kinds of diets, from the most flexible to the borderline sadistic; from the dungeon-type variety to those that evoke the tropical charms of South Beach.

Why such a fuss?

Women submit to such extremes of torture in order to fit into the shape of a Jessica Alba, while men –with less vanity, perhaps- give in to the fear of bad cholesterol, triglycerides and other extraterrestrial beings.

I don't know. It seems to me that Jessica (or any other squalid little diva) is more than the sum of the meager calories she absorbs every day. We should try to find some kind of balance between Miss Twiggy and Miss Piggy, don't you think? But try telling that to any American housewife. If you're obsessed with losing weight, you'll see yourself fat every time you take a look at the mirror.

As for cholesterol, who knows? My grandfather died at the age of 90, after being reasonably thin and healthful all his life. He never spied on his metabolism, and he never went on a diet either. Back where I came from, real men don't do that.

That said, I must admit I tried dieting once. Years go, when all my pants suddenly started to choke my belly, I followed a friend's advice. He told me his wife had come up with a recipe for some kind of magic veggie soup, with which you could lose at least 50 pounds in just a couple days. So I had that for breakfast, lunch and supper for a whole month. Then, one day I started feeling dizzy and weak. My wife led me, almost stumbling, all the way to the doctor.

After listening to my story and inquiring a bit about my symptoms, the good man —a doctor of the old Cuban school who also treated my mom and other relatives- scribbled something in his prescription pad and handed me the note. Fortunately, I read it right away, because clearly it wasn't meant for a drug store.

"What's this?"

"The medicine you need," the doctor said, smiling and showing us the way out.

My wife was curious and asked me to read the prescription for her when were back in the car: "Steak and fries. Take twice every day at the same time," it said.

Please don't change too much

THIS COUNTRY WILL CHANGE YOU inevitably. There's no avoiding that. It either multiplies the virtues you already have or forces you to do a big turnaround. Resistance is useless —and may be lethal, too. It's called survival, in case you don't know.

As a newcomer, I was fortunate enough to follow a path akin to my professional interests. I'm involved in journalism —certainly an ungrateful trade- but I can't complain. Others have not been as lucky.

A friend of mine arrived in America two years after I did. Back where we came from, he was an employee in the U.S. Embassy. I had always thought he would become a top banana in some company when he got here. Indeed, he had the talent. But I was flabbergasted when I bumped into him one day in Miami.

He was wearing a purple tunic, decorated with embroidered moons and stars, and he had shaved his head like a Buddhist monk straight out of the *Kung Fu* series. As he saw me, he joined the palms of his hands and leaned to greet me, quite ceremoniously. I couldn't stop laughing.

My friend explained that in this new incarnation his task was to offer prophecies and provide spiritual advice. He was publishing his predictions in a popular women's magazine, and he made some extra bucks by consulting out of his home. Apparently, he was doing well, but I would have never imagined him involved in such an esoteric trade. He had always been so practical.

"You have to make a living here, Manny," he said, fighting to straighten his tunic.

Another acquaintance of mine was a well-known stylist back where we came from. With his skills, he always led a good life there. He had quite a long list of clients among performing artists. But when he arrived in America he realized competition was very tough in his line of business. There are plenty of stylists around, and if you can't dish out enough money to pay for a TV ad, you're screwed.

"What else could I do?" He said, with a touch of sadness, the day we bumped into each other.

He certainly didn't lack clients now, but the ones he had weren't very talkative, and if by any chance he pulled their hair the wrong way, they would bite him.

My friend was working now in the thriving pet industry, in a segment they call pet grooming. The animals he cared for were all very different, from those with kinky hair to those who hardly needed any brushing. They all barked, and none offered a tip for services. What a way to make a living!

I thank God for my professional blessings every time I hear of cases like these. In America, you almost always prevail, though often not in a field of your own choosing. You change, but not necessarily the way you'd want to. At times, I'm afraid, you undergo quite a dramatic metamorphosis.

Who could have predicted that a writer friend of mine, an exquisite poet, would end as a *capo* of organized crime after arriving in America? We met by chance in one the many parties and black tie events they're always throwing in Miami. He was dressed very elegantly –I think Armani- and was surrounded by at least half a dozen bodyguards wearing dark glasses. When he noticed my surprise, he confided, in whispers, the dark source of his fortune.

Tired of just dreaming and writing verse, the poet decided to embark on a more lucrative career laundering money back in the wild 80's. At some point, he avoided doing jail time and got to keep a lot of money by making a deal with the authorities. So now he went by another name and enjoyed the protection of that safety detail, to prevent some hitman from shooting him dead.

I nodded and quietly walked away from him, under the pretext of finding some tasty *hors d'oeuvres* they were passing around. Call me a coward if you will, but I'm in no way addicted to lead. After surviving for so many years without having to make predictions, brush doggy hair or launder money, I felt no urgent need to tempt fate. You only live once –even in America.

Welcome to the land of trash

THE FIRST COLOR TV we owned in this country came straight out of the trash. Weed was growing inside it; I can't imagine why. I picked it up in some backyard. When I plugged it in for the first time, I had serious doubts it would work, but its screen miraculously lit up. In a matter of seconds we were watching a rerun of *Fantasy Island!*

As a newcomer, I heard people tell me money didn't grow on trees in this country. That's certainly true, but judging by how much stuff gets thrown away every single day here, you'd think everything is free in America.

Back where I came from, many even keep empty soda cans as souvenirs; they think they look cute on the living room coffee table. Here, however, the usefulness of any object is quite ephemeral. The minute it shows any signs of malfunction, or we simply become bored with it, we just throw it away mercilessly, like garbage.

Repair a broken stereo or electric iron? Forget it. Better buy yourself a new one; it's going to be cheaper. And in the process, you help push the economy ahead, especially if you have no other choice but to use your good credit.

Maybe you don't remember, but back in the town where I came from –and probably in yours, too- there were plenty of shoe repairmen, TV mechanics, scissor sharpeners… and even people who would make your old bed's box spring feel like brand new. In America, all these people would have dropped their trades and would be probably living on welfare.

I don't know about you, but it still saddens me to throw away an old stereo just because a small piece of wiring in it broke, or because I bought myself a new one. It makes me sad, too, to throw away a five-year-old computer just to make space for another one with a larger memory or some other nicety they were offering out there.

There used to be charitable organizations that took care of these objects in their old age, but these days it seems that even compassion has shifted gears. When we were moving from New York and needed to get rid of some old stuff, a well-known charitable organization even inquired about the brands involved and how old the items were. In the end, they didn't show to pick them up. What could we do about it? I wonder if these people still take cash donations.

Don't get me wrong. I'm not one of those sentimental fellows who are in the habit of hoarding things. For me, life is not a journey requiring many souvenirs. A reasonable number of photos and a handful of papers should be enough to document my simple existence. But it happens that I grow attached to certain things, especially electronics and cars.

I once had to deliver a vehicle I had driven for about six years to a dealership where I was buying a new car with a trade-in. I almost cried, honestly. All of a sudden, I remembered all the places that very reliable car had taken me —and so safely! It just wasn't fair to drop it off just like that.

In the apartment we left behind, back where we came from, there was an American-made refrigerator. It was so old that my parents had used it to keep the milk I was fed when I was still communicating in baby talk. Later, it cooled our water and preserved our food when I was an adult —and my own kid's milk, too. In America, it would probably qualify as a museum piece.

In sum, even in this age of frenzied consumerism, I dare to demand a little more respect for those useful objects that surround us. Those old gadgets that served us so well at all hours of day, that bonded so much with our families over time, don't deserve a fate as horrible as the city dump. I'll admit they are inanimate beings, but I'm sure inside their plastic and metal entrails, a friendly, familiar heart beats for us.

By the way, I wonder whatever happened to that TV set with the weed growing inside. For the life of me, I can't remember exactly when we threw it away.

Never trust prizes that come in the mail

MY FRIEND CALLED EARLY. Too early, I might add, since I was brushing my teeth and getting ready to take off for work. I almost couldn't understand what he was saying. He was euphoric. I asked him to calm down and explain what was going on.

"I won a big prize," he said, finally. "Ten million dollars!"

I'll admit I was alarmed. At that time, most of those games weren't legal in our state, and anyhow, my friend didn't have the money to place any bets. I thought he had gone suddenly nuts and needed help quickly –perhaps of the 911 kind.

"Are you sure?" I asked, cautiously.

"Of course," he said. "I just got a letter in the mail."

I thought about it for a moment. Even as a newcomer, I started getting all kinds of crazy offers in the mail. I can't imagine how those people –whoever they were- found out I had just arrived in

Key West, but not a week went by that I didn't get a whole bunch of ads, flyers, magic crucifixes —and even the good news that I had won one prize or another.

I didn't want to drop a bucket of cold water on my friend. God knows newcomers need all the encouragement they can get. So I asked him, again very cautiously, if he had sent an entry to any contest recently. He told me that he hadn't.

"Have you read the whole letter?" I asked him then.

He was silent. Short but long silent, if you know what I mean. Then, he hung up abruptly. I assumed my friend had realized the truth and had become very disappointed. As a matter of routine, in America, you must be very skeptical of anything you get in the mail —especially 10-million-dollar prizes you have just won.

The truth is con artists are everywhere. But in America some of them actually have a license to deceive the public. They say you won a huge prize, but barely two lines later they tell you why you can't collect it. That's what fine print was designed for, to tell you in a whisper what every smart person should know.

The bottom line is you will never get a huge jackpot in the mail. You'll always be required to buy something, answer three or four quick questions, or maybe attend a seminar in some distant hotel, where you will always be greeted by a smiling salesperson.

One time, I got one of those amazing letters myself. It stated I had won one of three prizes —a trip to Costa Rica, a brand new car or a romantic dinner for two in a five-star hotel, limousine included. To make my choice, I just had to call a certain phone number.

I dialed right away. At the time, as a newcomer, I was not too good at detecting crooks. I wanted the brand new car, definitely. A Cadillac if it was possible. Fortunately, when the sweet voice on the other end of the line told me I would need to send $50 for a processing fee required in Detroit, it all became clear to me.

So much money for a car I hadn't even seen yet? Forget it.

Looking back, it was the best thing I could do. Apparently many don't know this, but just living in this country, rife with opportunities and with swindlers as well, is enough of a prize. All other windfalls –the ones that come in the mail or insinuate themselves in a phone call- are just tricks designed for fools. Believe me, the fruits of hard work are the only jackpot here.

Why do you need a watch if you don't have time?

I HAVE LITTLE TIME, or none at all. Sometimes I ask myself why do I even need a watch. Why count the hours and the minutes if, in the end, they don't truly belong to you?

As a newcomer, I assumed simplistically I had just made a change of residence. What I actually did was to jump from a slow, ceremonious merry-go-round to another one that gyrates fast and furiously, in a non-stop ride. Or could it be, perhaps, an out-of control roller coaster?

I don't know about you, but I still remember that back where I came from there was always time to do lots of things besides working. We had visitors at home at any hour, and right then and there a lunch or supper was improvised for them. Every once in a while, we went out for a walk with friends or acquaintances. We walked, we talked, we philosophized endlessly –and we even had time to go to sleep early.

I suppose this probably sounds very provincial, but I still miss the slow, elastic kind of time we enjoyed back where I came from. The moment you arrive in America, it seems like a bunch of tasks fall on you –work, of course, but also shopping, the kids' school, things that need to be fixed around home, writing checks, visiting the doctor, whatever.

Some years ago, after a particularly long wait, an old friend of ours finally realized his dream of coming to America. We were very glad when we heard he had arrived, and almost right away I managed to get his phone number from somebody, and gave him a call.

I realized he was living very close to us, barely a half-hour away. He was staying for the moment with some cousins. We had a great talk over the phone, exchanging gossip and old memories. It's amazing all the things that seem to happen as soon as you take off for another country –weddings, engagements, divorces, fights, kids are born to the most unlikely couples... It's like dying without all the tears and the funeral. Our friend put us up to date on everything. Then, we agreed we would meet sometime. I am still waiting.

Each time I called him, it seemed he had to do one thing or another, from some urgent paperwork at the Social Security office to taking the test for his driver's license. I thought we'd be able to meet as soon as he began to drive and found a job, but it didn't happen. The more he became immersed in his new life, the more difficult it was to meet. One day, by chance, we bumped into him in the supermarket, and we finally embraced in person. Months later, his cousins told me he had moved to another state, where he had found a better job.

I don't know why you are always so short of time in America. Just paying your bills seems like a full-time job. You need the smarts of a good accountant to balance your checkbook here, too. There are always so many deposits, expenses and obligations to track.

Doing your shopping involves, for example, an exceptional sense of logistics –take advantage of the sales, be prudent with your use of credit, and especially, devote almost an entire day to those purchases. Not to mention the stupid car: if it breaks down, you're as good as dead.

And on top of that, you must take turns to get your vacations at work.

I understand there are experts now that help people to manage their time. In this country, there's an expert for almost everything. According to them, in order to keep control you only need to prioritize certain tasks. It seems simple, but considering how many seemingly important things you usually have to do around here I find this to be a pointless exercise.

Why worry if you don't have time to worry? Better close your eyes and take your foot off the pedal –if you can.

Be careful with Uncle Sam's help

FEW PEOPLE ARE truly poor in America. Don't get me wrong. I'm not saying everyone's rich here. But while some do go through very hard times in this country, the prevailing safety net allows many to be indigent and yet enjoy the comforts of air conditioning and even cable TV.

As a newcomer more than 20 years ago, I thought poor people in America went around pushing carts and begging for money, being basically homeless. Just the thought we could end up like that made me very scared.

But a very circumspect government official proved me wrong. After handing us our refugee documents, he explained we would soon start getting food stamps, medical care, and English-language crash courses —all free of charge.

So just days after arriving in America, instead of begging for money, we found ourselves shopping and having to choose between a can of black beans and one of fruit cocktail. Every time we had to go to the hospital, we would present a red plastic card they had given us. Doctors took good care of us and prescribed medications to make us healthy again. Uncle Sam paid all the bills.

At first, I thought this was like manna from heaven; but soon I began to realize all this generosity actually came at a very high price –that of being watched all the time, relentlessly. Have you ever heard of Big Brother?

Once in a while, we would get these very long forms in the mail. We had to fill them out and return them right away; otherwise, they warned us, we would lose our benefits. The forms were complex and at times we could barely understand them. If you needed an explanation, you were supposed to call a number that was busy most of the time. To amuse you while they put you on hold, they made you listen to a long string of instrumental music.

How much money did you make in the last three months? Is someone other than yourself helping you pay the rent? Do you have a bank account? Do you own stock, have life insurance? Are your parents alive? The questionnaire was so long it took hours to fill it out, and at times you felt like giving just one simple answer: None of your business. But normally, you try to keep quiet when you are needy.

My only consolation was that in time we would be able to shed those uncomfortable little perks. What really puzzled me was that other newcomers clung so hard to them, even to the point of lying to retain them, once they were on their own feet. Every time they went to the welfare office and they got their food stamps, they would come out jumping and smiling. Poor devils.

As for me, one of the most joyous moments of my life in this country was when I finally called in to say we would not need any further assistance. That didn't stop them from putting me on hold, but I was nevertheless happy. I had just got a job that paid reasonably well and I asked them to close our case.

The employee on the other end of the line was speechless.

"Are you really sure?" He asked, finally.

"Quite sure, sir," I said.

Having made some calculations based on our new income, the employee had concluded that even now we were eligible to receive about $20 in cash assistance every month, as well as a small amount in food stamps.

"Never mind, it's OK," I said. I couldn't wait to throw away all those long forms I had been filling out and getting our lives back.

And so, just by hanging up the phone, my brief relationship with the Welfare State came to an end. I must admit the government help did serve a purpose for us at first. We're still thankful for it. But it's not really good to get used to those handouts. I know of some who arrived more or less at the same time we did, and they still seem to qualify for them. Apparently, all the effort they put into preserving this "aid" left them without the time or the will to move ahead.

That said, every time I have to visit the doctor these days, and I have to pay the bill, I remember that blessed red plastic card they gave us once.

There's room for everyone

I MUST BE A VERY WEIRD kind of Latino. I simply love American oldies music and still have fond memories of being some sort of a hippie back in the Havana of the 60's. Can you imagine?

With my deepest apologies to Beny Moré, Pérez Prado and all the saints of Cuban music, neither rumba nor salsa were made for me. If you really want to see me dancing and shaking my bones all over the place, you better provide yourself and your party's DJ with all those great hits by Elvis and Neal Sedaka, the Beatles and the Stones.

Now that's great music.

Never mind *danzón* and *guaracha,* and forget about the cha-cha, too. Even if my skin is brown and I'll take Spanish over English any time, the compass in my heart and my feet has always pointed up north. So as a newcomer in America I had to challenge many stereotypes.

Are you Cuban? Wow, you must be a salsa master then. And by the way, did you ever meet Desi Arnaz?

In social situations, I have often found myself dealing very tactfully with these difficult questions. You don't want to hurt anybody's feelings or needlessly cause disappointment. I usually refuse to make a demonstration of my *guarachero* expertise under the pretext of a sudden back pain. I tell them Desi was a distant cousin of mine, but I never had the honor of meeting him.

Ay, ay, ay!

When I arrived in America, I thought I had come to the land of a thousand dances. But I soon realized many of my compatriots were entrenched in an incurable musical nostalgia. As for the rest of Hispanics, most of them had an idealized version of us. They all perceived us as maraca-wielding people, which didn't come as a surprise to me. Hollywood has always depicted us in that funny way.

I suppose something similar happens often to many Mexicans and Argentineans who have moved here. Lots of people believe they're instantly qualified to intone a *corrido* or to dance a perfect tango just because of their nationality. They're either *charros* or *gauchos*. I get to be Arnaz. I guess it's unavoidable.

Years ago, when I was living in Miami, my car broke down in the middle of a street. I had to slowly push it to a service station close by. The owner's face looked familiar to me.

"Hey, I know you," he said the minute I walked into his office.

He was an old buddy from my high school days in Cuba. He was fatter and had grown a big moustache, but his eyes and smile hadn't changed at all. The radio in his office was tuned in to one of my favorite stations. A Four Seasons song was playing, and as we listened to it, we conjured memories of the good old times. The girls at school, all the struggle to keep our long hair…

"Know what?" He said then. "The first Friday of every month a whole bunch of us gets together in the evening. Want to come?"

He offered me a flyer in Spanish, with psychedelic letters, flowers and colorful mandalas splashed all over it. I couldn't believe it. It was the same group from my happy days as a teenager, and they had even found themselves a DJ to bring music to their monthly meetings.

Too bad I never attended. Quite frankly, the paper kept me very busy at the time, and I didn't want to start feeling like a senior either. It was too early for that, I thought. But this experience revealed something you have probably already found out for yourselves: in America, there's room for everyone.

Even for those old Latino hippies that, for some reason or another, never learned to do the salsa.

If the worst happens, don't despair

I HOPE IT NEVER HAPPENS to you. No matter what they say, no one is ready to be laid off, or as they say now, *downsized*.

You'll know what I'm talking about if you get the pink slip some day. I've never quite understood why your last check is supposed to be that color, because that moment is anything but rosy. The same goes for the green card, which isn't that color anymore, but they still call it that way. Could it be it stands for hope?

Anyway, as a newcomer I was tremendously happy when I got my first job in America. Every time I bumped into an old acquaintance I shared the good news: I have a job! I have a job! But then, someone gave me a reality check.

"There's nothing secure here," he said. "The day you least expect it they'll give you a layoff."

"What's that?" I asked.

What he told me sounded so strange and cruel to me: just a few weeks after he started working with a small firm, he was called to the manager's office and was informed that they were letting him go.

It was not that he was a bad employee. His skills and dedication were not in question and, in fact, the company was recommending him highly. However, they needed to cut their staff.

This crushed me emotionally. I felt like a kid who's just found out there's no Santa and that his parents may disown him at any time. How could anyone commit such an injustice? There ought to be a law about this, I thought.

But, as they say here, s__t happens. Two years later, I found myself facing the head of human resources in the publishing house with which I was working at the time, a good-natured Italian guy who tried to explain things to me as best he could.

The company was in financial trouble due to the Mexican peso crisis, and since I was one of the last to be hired, they were *terminating* my position. I tried to remain calm, but no matter how much you prepare yourself for it, you feel like screaming, crying, kicking —especially if they tell you your performance is great and it has nothing to do with you getting kicked out.

In fact, together with the bad news, the company gave me an excellent letter of recommendation as well as a check equivalent to two weeks' pay. Quite little, considering back in the 80's I had a whole life ahead of me, a family to support and, of course, bills to pay.

So in a short time, we were back where we started —in Miami. We were also at the complete mercy of unemployment compensation, which would not last forever. Would we end up living in the streets?

I collected my benefits for a couple of months, while I applied for jobs all over Miami, a town that looked much somber to me each day. Until finally, after making many promises to Saint Jude, an old friend in local radio called me up to work with him in a news segment he was going to start running –and he offered a better salary than the one I had before, too!

From that job I jumped to a better one, and since then I haven't been laid off again.

So you see: Sometimes good things come from the bad. Don't despair.

The hunt for the magic 'tripisoo'

DRESSING UP FOR A JOB interview is like dressing up for a funeral or a wedding. Are you overdressed? Should your suit be dark or light? Will this tie make a good impression? There are lots of questions and very few answers.

You see, fashion isn't exactly one of my fortes, and as much as I'd want to, I'm sure I'll never become an expert in workplace etiquette, nor in any other kind of etiquette for that matter. I'm just that kind of guy.

As a newcomer, I used to turn up for job interviews wearing modest blue jeans and a simple T-shirt. What the heck, for the kind of job I was looking for –basically one that would help to pay a few bills- I figured I didn't need any fancy suit.

But then, one day someone told me I needed to buy a *tripisoo*. I didn't ask what that was. At that time, I kept discovering simple things every day –doors that quietly opened themselves when you faced them and faucets from which water started flowing just by showing them your hands. People stared at me with a mix of mockery and compassion. What could I do?

So one morning I went out hunting for a *tripisoo*. The word brought to my mind one of those sweet Italian desserts, but it turned out to be something you don't eat but rather wear. A baker in the neighborhood kindly explained the real meaning to me the day before, as he bagged the guava turnovers I had just ordered. "Three... piece... suit," he recited, very slowly.

Duh. Only then I realized what it was.

I had seen many of those —blue, gray, striped. My boss wore a different one every day, and you could see them all the time in the movies, where the main characters were always attorneys, gangsters or tycoons. I saw them advertised in the papers, too, but they cost a fortune. Where would I get the money to buy one?

My job interview was scheduled for next week. I was shooting for a position in a radio station's newsroom. Indeed, this seemed a bit more serious than the job I had at the time, where the only etiquette was not to go buck-naked, if you know what I mean. Someone advised me to go to a discount store located just minutes from where I lived. They assured me they had lots of *tripisoos* for sale there.

An employee who noticed me nosing around asked me what I was looking for, and I told him right away: A cheap, nice-looking *tripisoo*. I didn't mention quality, of course, considering the measly $60 I had for that very important purchase.

The employee looked me over thoughtfully.

"A *tripisoo* like this one may be a good investment," he said, showing me a light brown one that hung close by.

Usually, he would recommend dark blue for a job interview. "It shows authority," he explained. But considering the local hot weather, as well as my personality, his guess was that a light-colored one would work better for me.

Frankly, I didn't know what he was talking about. I had been raised on the notion that people are more than just than the sum of the clothes they wear, but judging by what he was saying, I had been probably wrong all along.

"Do you think with this suit I will get the job I want?" I asked, doubtfully.

"Why, of course," the guy said. He went on to explain the magic properties that suit apparently had, and how the minute he set his eyes on it, any manager would want to hire me.

"How do you think I got this job?" He asked, gesturing toward the whole store, very much like a monarch would show you his kingdom.

I paid the 60 bucks and left.

My job interview was actually very short. After a couple of clumsy answers on my part, the hiring manager courteously told me he would be in touch. I never saw him again.

However, that *tripisoo* proved good for two or three more interviews, and one of them was a successful one. Later, over the years, it began to wear out. It just didn't look that good anymore, so I gave it to a newcomer who was looking for a job. I don't know if it worked out for him.

There's always a first time

WE HAVE LIVED FOR more than 20 years in this country. Recently, it was our 27th anniversary. That's quite a long time, but you often don't realize it. My wife had to remind me about it, as of many other things.

As a newcomer, I never took the trouble of keeping count of the time that would inevitably distance us completely from our native land and allow us to grow roots in America. Now I do sometimes. It's a moment to look back and reflect.

Once in a while, I ask myself what would have been of us if we hadn't taken that bold step, coming here. Would we have ever resigned ourselves to our fate back there? Would we be still pondering whether to leave or stay?

It's hard to know. And besides, who cares?

I spent my first years in America in a state of near-permanent amazement.

One of the first things that caught my curiosity was the hot water. I'm not talking about the one you boil in a pot, or the one you warm up by turning on a gas heater minutes before taking a bath, like we used to do back "home". I'm talking about continuous, 24/7, hot water, the kind you enjoy almost everywhere in this country.

I must admit that for some time I failed to understand where this miracle of modern comfort originated. It wasn't until I bought a home that I realized all that water went through a cylindrical electric heater, hidden somewhere in the house, that kept it like that, very warm, day and night.

On the opposite side of temperatures, the omnipresence of air conditioning was another delightful surprise for me.

Back where I came from, air conditioning was just an exceptional advantage, the kind you usually found in some stores, theaters and government offices. "Climatized" —that's what they called it proudly. The rest of us had to rely on the breeze or maybe a fan to fight off the heat.

Here, just pushing a tiny lever is enough to turn on a powerful engine that will instantly placate the rigors of summer. The average Joe has this wonderful contraption at his disposal all the time —as long as he pays the humongous electric bills that keeping the house cool usually involves.

A couple years after I arrived, I discovered microwave ovens. I had seen them displayed in some stores, but I had postponed buying one after an acquaintance warned me one of those things could paralyze my heart if I didn't watch out. Fortunately, I later learned the warning was only meant for people who had a pacemaker implanted. My heart worked fine. So I went to buy a microwave oven right away.

It was great! We could heat our water, our milk and our meals without actually using fire. I didn't even care how it worked. Every time we had someone for a visit, I would show my new gadget as proudly as if it was some Sèvres porcelain vase or Picasso's *Guernica.*

Some years later, I lost interest, and the microwave oven slipped quietly into oblivion, just like had happened with the color TV and the stereo before. I suppose it sounds a bit cold-hearted, but what the heck. Habit does kill passion, you know.

I guess we all have some funny story to tell about the first steps we took in America. I do too. I, too, was very clumsy and naïve at first. But at least I didn't try talking to a soda vending machine, like I've been told some newcomers did.

However, I do remember putting once a pizza in the oven – box, wrapper and all- thinking I was following all the directions to a T.

There's always a first time.

Seeking the Fountain of Youth... again

THEY SAY JUAN PONCE DE LEÓN came to this land long ago seeking the Fountain of Youth. But as much as he skinny-dipped in the ponds, lakes and rivers he found on his way through Florida, he never recovered the freshness and the energy of his younger age. We are told he finally died by the poison of an Indian arrow. Poetic justice, I suppose

This is a sad story many feel apparently compelled to repeat these days. If you have not realized it by now, America is totally obsessed with the myth of eternal youth. The commercials on TV and the newspaper ads keep touting all sorts of remedies for wrinkles, blemishes, varicose veins and all those nice things that usually come with old age. This country has also become like a Mecca for plastic surgeons.

As a newcomer, I was only about 30 years old, so I didn't worry much about looking younger. No one really wants to look like a baby, I'm sure. My mom did warn me, however, that I shouldn't be too candid about my age.

"Always try to shave off a couple years," she advised. "You should start early. It's not good to be old here."

I thought she was just exaggerating, but when I learned that in America you become a part of a "protected class" the moment you turn 40, I started worrying every time I saw a tiny speck of white showing in my head.

Back where I came from, people in their forties or fifties are considered "relatively young". In this country, being such an age would make you almost a senior, or place you, as some would say, definitely over the hill.

Being a part of a "protected class" sort of keeps you on the edge most of the time, especially because all the forms you have to fill –and there are many- require you to clearly state your date of birth at one point or another.

An employee who's close to retirement age drives up the costs of health insurance for a company, according to some. Also, since he's been on the job for such a long time, penny-pinching managers would argue he makes too much money. Come layoff time, he's usually one of the first to go. So it should come as no surprise that millions continue the hunt for the Fountain of Youth way beyond Florida. It's a matter of survival in this country.

I'll admit my wife managed to convince me of dyeing my hair several times, but I've never lied about my age in America, at least not in any of the forms I have filled. A friend once told me he almost ended up in jail for doing that. Why run the risk? True, America worships youth. But it worships honesty even more – and you better not forget that.

Meanwhile, plastic surgeons are thriving here. They straighten out wrinkles, siphon off the extra grease, and give you Botox shots here and there. For some patients, surgery is not an option anymore, because they've had so many. If they just try to smile, it seems like the skin on their cheeks is going to explode. To put your spirits high there's Viagra and other magic potions, too.

Is it worth it? I don't really know. But I prefer to show my white hair instead of pretending I'm a teenager. In this country, and in any other, there's only one way not to grow old –and that's to die young. And you probably know by now how expensive funerals can be in America.

What can we do with this alligator?

WE'VE BEEN NEIGHBORS with this alligator for a couple weeks now. Well, not really an alligator, not yet. It's just a little one, a baby, if you will. It is small, yes, but it's nevertheless endowed with the sharp teeth, the beady eyes and the swirling tail of a regular, adult alligator. You know, that typical Florida native.

One afternoon, the alligator quietly established residence in the artificial lake that graces the very center of our apartment complex. We have no idea how it slipped in. As many other reptiles, it probably has the skills of a professional contortionist.

The apartment complex management absolutely refuses to touch it. They claim it's a protected species and they could be fined for messing with it. Animal Control, on the other hand, insists there's nothing it can do either, at least until this animal grows to be five feet long. That's little consolation for us, of course.

As a newcomer, I soon realized the deep respect in which most of Americans hold the subjects of the animal kingdom. Even if it's admirable, it never ceases to puzzle me.

Many cats and dogs lead handsome lives here, while some human beings simply go hungry. In the streets, you can see owners following their pets with a plastic bag, ready to pick up the poop after they're done. Meanwhile, some municipalities have declared war on the homeless.

Why such a disparity?

I suppose it's some sort of misplaced compassion. Animals are like orphans. If you don't care for these helpless creatures, who is going to do it? A whole industry thrives on this, producing tons of canned food, special medications, toys and even clothing for all these fortunate beasts.

As for human beings, they're all supposed to act like adults and to bear responsibility for themselves. If for some reason you are unable to find a job and make an honest living, the only right you have is to fend for yourself as best you can.

Not that we're necessarily more compassionate back where I came from. There are plenty of beggars around. Poverty is widespread, but at least animals have their fair share of it. Very few dogs and cats are totally happy over there, I'm sure.

I bring all this up because I've become very concerned about this alligator roaming around our home. After scaring away all the cute little ducks that swam in the lake, it has decided to take naps close to the pool, in plain sight of our terrace.

It also seems many children have grown fond of it and they're now feeding it pieces of bread and hot dog leftovers all the time. Soon, if they go on like that, the alligator will get fatter and stronger. What will we do with it, when it's four feet long and has grown teeth as long as knives?

I have no idea.

Back where I came from, I'd be going around with a shotgun up on my shoulder, ready to turn this stupid reptile into purse material. But here such a behavior would probably lead to jail time and raise a public outcry.

Sometimes, I'm under the impression human beings aren't the most favored species in this country. The government charges us a fee for protection, pretty much like the Mafia does; but it refuses to defend us when we most need it. What can we do about it? We'll just have to get used to the alligator.

Who does he think he is? A doctor?

Y EARS AGO, WHEN I was still battling to get a driver's
license, I was standing in line in a Department of Motor
Vehicles office, when a newcomer just like me started
telling me all about his struggles and disappointments.

Poor guy. Apparently, things were not going too well for him.
He had not found a job yet, and he could barely afford to pay the
rent for his small apartment. He had failed so far to reinsert
himself in his profession. He was a teacher, I think. Fortunately, I
had already found a job myself so I was able offer him some
quick advice.

"Don't sell yourself cheap," I said. "Knowing you're a
newcomer, they'll offer you the lowest salary. Don't jump on it."

At that moment, a young Hispanic lady who was in line ahead
of us turned toward her companion and commented in English
how irritating all these "new arrivals" were to her. No job was
good enough for them, and they were mostly lazy and ignorant,

according to her. Then she raised her little nose, pointing it at us disdainfully.

"Who does he think he is? A doctor?" She protested loudly.

I rarely pay attention to the small indignities life brings my way every day. My wife thinks I'm just too civil. But I took exception this time, perhaps because the comments involved not only me, but also a fellow newcomer who was going through hard times. And since I was lucky enough to understand English, I just felt the urgent need to retort, "Yes, young lady, I happen to be a doctor. And what are you? A waitress, by any chance?"

The poor girl was livid. Her companion stiffened by her side, visibly ready for action. He was a tall, muscular kind of fellow. We eyed each other angrily, but it didn't go beyond that. A security guard intervened quickly, to prevent a potential fistfight.

"Please, doctor," he pleaded with me.

I almost laughed.

I don't know what's wrong with us immigrants. We tend to be so patronizing toward those who have arrived in this country just a while before us. We scold them all the time, as if they were newborns, and not simply newcomers. Sometimes I think we just see in them a reflection of our own clumsy past. Who knows? They probably perceive us as strange creatures, too.

As a newcomer, for example, it was very hard for me to understand why people in this country treasured so many trivial possessions. They held their rugs, record players and TV sets in such high esteem, and boasted so much of the car or the blender they had just bought! How silly, I thought. But now I actually do the same. Why are we like that?

Anyway, I've never forgotten the incident with that young lady, or the answer I shot at her. I'm pretty sure she remembers it, too. Looking back, I probably overreacted, but I think I did the right thing anyway.

The truth is in this country you must always set yourself higher goals. If you don't actually believe you deserve the best, then you will end up deserving nothing.

You should never sell yourself cheap, and never hesitate to exaggerate your value whenever it seems convenient. You see, in this country, hype is king. We all have to become our own spokesperson at one time or another.

Sometimes, the candidate who's more qualified doesn't necessarily get the job, but actually the one who pretends to know the most. You don't need to lie, just put yourself where you truly belong. Take it from me: I'm no doctor.

How easy you get used to good things

NOT TOO LONG AGO, the air conditioning quit on us. I woke up very sweaty and jumped from bed with the funny notion I would fix whatever was wrong with it, but it was useless. Instead of cooling the house, the darn thing only blew out waves of hot, thick steam. I had to turn it off. I quickly went to break the bad news to my wife:

"The air broke down."

This would seem quite a mundane incident anywhere, but try doing without air conditioning in Florida for a single day of summer. The Devil himself would not tolerate it, let alone a mere human being. It's a catastrophe.

As a newcomer, I remained for some time a typical creature of the Tropics. I mean, I didn't go around smiling all the time, wearing shorts and a Hawaiian shirt combination, while happily shaking my *maracas,* as we're usually depicted in the travel books.

But I still remember how easy it was for me to endure hot weather shortly after I arrived in America. I've had practice.

If you're like me, where you came from, few houses have central air conditioning. Am I wrong? No one has even thought of installing air conditioning in cars and public buses either. At best, the driver wears a small towel over his neck, and for cool air he relies on waving a folded newspaper.

South of the border, cold air is decidedly for tourists. That's why you always find it in five-star hotels and also in those beautiful shiny buses that shuttle visitors around, like cool islands floating in a tepid, sticky sea.

It may be that coldness is the best measure for social development. In America, people take for granted what García Márquez famously called in one of his novels "the cold stone" – ice, that is. In the rest of the planet –maybe with the exception of the North Pole- every time you order a soda you must clearly tell the waiter you want it "iced". Otherwise, you'll get it straight out of the fridge, but not as cold as you'd probably want it.

Why is that?

Once, as I sat quietly in a restaurant facing the old colonial area of Santo Domingo, I decided to order a very cold beer. No matter what season it is, it can get real hot in the Dominican Republic. So I thought I would get my beer as cold and brittle as snow. But the one the waiter brought for me was barely colder than the 90+ degrees we were enjoying that morning –or at least it appeared to be that way. I always tend to exaggerate a bit.

"Don't you have a colder one?" I asked the waiter.

"Oh," he said, "You want it *ceniza*," meaning "ashen" in Spanish.

"Yes, very *ceniza*, please," I told him.

Since then, I always ask for my beer that way –at least every time I'm in Santo Domingo. *Ceniza* is good for there. In other places, I use some different word that indicates extreme glacial cold.

I tell you al this because the day my wife and I had to endure without air conditioning was even worse than the "day without Mexicans" some wanted to inflict on the Gringos some time ago. I thought we were going to melt, honestly. To make things worse, it was a Sunday, so we could expect little help from the building management.

So we dug out an old electric fan and put it to good use. In the evening, we did as we used to do back "home": we both sat in the terrace to kill time talking and reading, away from the TV set and the computer that normally absorb so much of our precious life together.

Of course, we could have driven earlier to the mall as well, but somehow the idea didn't appeal to either of us. The weather was so hot we felt practically paralyzed.

It's amazing how easy you get used to good things.

Toxic anniversaries

A ND BY THE WAY, WHEN did you arrive in the States?"
It's a question I've been asked very often. For some reason, the date of admission into this exclusive club that goes by the acronym USA carries a huge weight on the perception some people may have of us.

As a newcomer, I used to answer the question quietly and very frankly, counting the months or the years with scrupulous accuracy. Later on, however, I tried my best to avoid it, or took the liberty of playing around with the exact date whenever I could.

Why?

I haven't figured that one out yet, but this is a hard question indeed, some sort of a riddle, because the answer can bring very bad consequences sometimes. Believe me: a greater or lesser degree of seniority in America can make a big difference for many of us.

Anyway, I was trying to do just that –to avoid or embellish- because at that very moment the one asking the hard question was none other than a top executives of one of America's oldest and most renowned publishing companies.

We were both having dinner in one of Manhattan's most prestigious clubs, too, for the exclusive use of Princeton alumni, and I was interviewing for a highly coveted position in his company.

"By the way, Manny, when did you arrive in the States?" He asked, casually.

I swallowed hard. The position for which I was interviewing was the top one in one of the oldest Spanish-language publications in America –and known all over the world, too. Not only an excellent salary was at stake, but a splendorous new line in my resume, I was sure. I simply couldn't afford to play dumb this time.

Besides, for some reason I trusted this executive to be an enlightened kind of person, someone who would not be prejudiced against my humble roots and the modest vessel that had carried me to these shores many years before. So I decided to come clean with him.

"Back in 1980," I said, finally. "On a shrimp boat. Do you remember Mariel?"

The executive, a man in his 50's at the time, seemed undisturbed. For a moment, he appeared to reflect and I assumed he was going to change the subject. But he suddenly frowned and simply said, *"Oh?"*

My friends: I'm sure you know Gringos well enough by now to understand the subtle difference between that exclamatory *"Oh!"* indicating thrill or surprise, and that other, question-marked *"Oh?"* expressing the most shocking, deepest disappointment.

Right away, I knew I had given the wrong answer. I should have said "1979" or "1978", any other year, excepting that one. What difference could it make?

In that gentleman's eyes, I had suddenly morphed into Tony Montana, the main character in that excellent Brian de Palma film, *Scarface,* which follows a *marielito's* bloody exploits as a gangster. Montana had arrived in America, pretty much like me, aboard a shrimp boat, in that fateful year, 1980. At that very moment I almost heard myself echoing Al Pacino's words in the movie, "I want my human rights now!"

The interview went all the way south at that critical point, of course. We spoke about almost everything, from how terrible the weather was those days, to –what else- the sorry state of subway transportation in New York. We finally said goodbye with a terse *"we'll be in touch",* but I never heard of him again. In short, I didn't get the job.

Some anniversaries can be toxic.

The one thing I regret

I WAS ALMOST BORN IN New York. Can you imagine? But it was my father's fault that I came into this world in Havana, instead. After so many years, I hate blaming him for him that, but it's the honest truth.

Shortly before I was born, my mom told me, my dad's feet got full of blisters. That winter, the streets of New York were soaked with rain and snow and slush, which caused the disease. They had both traveled to the Big Apple to take some post-graduate courses, and they had met and married there a year before.

Those days, there weren't so many over-the-counter remedies for athlete's foot available in U.S. pharmacies –at least not the one my dad urgently needed. The one he trusted was manufactured exclusively in Cuba at the time. Nowadays, he'd probably be able to order it in Miami or somewhere else, I'm sure; but by the end of the 40's the only stores that sold the miraculous Acetolia were in the island.

In any case, seeking relief for this seemingly mundane ailment, my parents traveled to Cuba just weeks before I was born. The rest, as they say, is history. I was born in a hospital located in El Cerro neighborhood, and that very much sealed my fate. You will probably think it's not a big deal. It made quite a difference for me, however.

I have asked myself many times how different my life would have been if my dad's feet wouldn't have gotten in the way; but I just hate to speculate about it. It's not fair. Fate always prevails, especially if it has already chosen a certain path for you. No one can alter that.

A painter friend of mine, for example, could not avoid the long years he had to wait until he was finally allowed to come to America, despite the fact he was born here and had a U.S. passport. There are mysteries that simply aren't worth pondering too much, except maybe if you are a philosopher –or something worse.

In any case, carrying a U.S. passport is and will remain the dream of many people in this world. To some, it basically falls on their lap; others, like me, must strive to win it. And with God's help, I was one of those fortunate enough to see their dream become a reality.

I have also asked myself lots of times if it was worth waiting so long, to leave so many dear people and things behind, to cross such a dangerous sea, to struggle so much, to adapt... Invariably, my answer is yes. And the reasons are numerous. Many, perhaps, will not share them, but as they often say in Spanish, "Different colors were made for different tastes."

Sometimes I've crossed paths with immigrants who see the lives they have led here with a mix of bitterness and disappointment. An acquaintance once told me he could have become a great performing artist back in his country, but he claimed his career had simply washed away in America, with the tiny, ethnic roles he had been forced to take in some movies.

I'll admit this country is no easy ride. Not many people are actually ready to face the multitude of demands that come from living in a country where money doesn't exactly grow on trees, as some tend to believe before they come here. Some careers can be very difficult to resurrect, too. The strong competition and the huge barrier posed by both language and culture may appear to be, at times, overwhelming.

Certainly, it's easier to thrive locally as a good auto mechanic than to become a top leader in the nation's transportation industry. Even the noblest of dreams face some limits. And yet, we know of some who do reach the very top –and then more. Who could have ever predicted Roberto Goizueta, a simple manager in a soda bottling plant in Cuba, would in time become the CEO of Coca-Cola, that very sacred American icon?

I count myself as lucky, having succeeded in finding a niche for myself in my profession, journalism, and reaching small but admirable heights in the process. I haven't won a Pulitzer so far, but every morning I went to my office in *The Wall Street Journal* I couldn't help remembering that barely 18 years before I had arrived in Key West with my wife and child, a single little suitcase, and of course, the hope of making a living doing almost anything. And there I was, in the Mecca of global financial publishing, nonetheless. Wouldn't you call that a dream?

True, I once also dreamed of becoming a poet, as good as my father was, and maybe even saw myself accepting the Nobel Prize for Literature at one point or another. In fact, I still write fiction in my free time, and now that I'm quietly slipping into retirement, I continue to harbor similar ambitions. Why not? I may even succeed at that before the game is over. But it will all depend, as with my professional success in America, on my own efforts and the will of God. I trust both.

That's exactly why when someone asks, pessimistically, if I don't regret having forsaken my native land in the quest for a mere illusion, or when someone bitterly suggests I could have done better back "home" than over here, or that this journey wasn't worth all the trouble, I'm quick to answer that not in my wildest dreams would I think of turning back. In fact, people, no

offense, but there's only one thing I regret at this point in my life
—not being born here.

Contents